THE LAWGIVERS

The LAWGIVERS

The Parallel Lives of
Numa Pompilius & Lycurgus of Sparta

AS TOLD BY PLUTARCH

Translated by C. Scot Hicks & David V. Hicks

CiRCE
Concord, NC

Published in the USA by the CiRCE Institute
© 2019 by C. Scot Hicks and David V. Hicks

ISBN: 978-0-9991466-8-2

All rights reserved. This publication may not be reproduced, stored in a retrieval system, or transmitted, in any form, or by any means, without the prior written consent of the CiRCE Institute.

For information:
CiRCE Institute
81 McCachern Blvd.
Concord, NC 28025
info@circeinstitute.com
www.circeinstitute.com

Cover design by Graeme Pitman.

Printed in the United States of America.

The CiRCE Institute is a non-profit 501(c)3 organization that exists to promote and support classical education in the school and in the home. We seek to identify the ancient principles of learning, to communicate them enthusiastically, and to apply them vigorously in today's learning settings through curriculum development, teacher training, leadership development events, online training, and a content-laden website.

To learn more please visit circeinstitute.org.

Using history as a mirror I try by whatever means I can to improve my own life and to model it by the standard of all that is best in those whose lives I write. As a result I feel as though I were conversing and indeed living with them; by means of history I receive each one of them in turn, welcome and entertain them as guests and consider their stature and their qualities and select from their actions the most authoritative and the best with a view to getting to know them. What greater pleasure could one enjoy than this or what more efficacious in improving one's own character?

—Plutarch, *Life of Timoleon*

CONTENTS

Foreword by Karen Glass i

An Introduction for Students New to Plutarch 1

A Note about the Translation 17

The Life of Lycurgus of Sparta 21

The Life of Numa Pompilius 91

Comparison of the Lawgivers Lycurgus & Numa 145

Bibliography 153

FOREWORD

by Karen Glass

If what we call classical education is a tradition, there are probably few things more traditional than the reading of *Plutarch's Lives*. His collection of "lives" linked the world of classical Greece to the Roman world in which he lived, and those lives have been read continuously ever since, especially by those who have taken their role as leaders seriously. These histories have been valuable to readers for centuries because they contain themes and ideas which are timeless. Many modern books are timely and worth reading because we want to stay abreast of current thought. However, it is only by reading the timeless works and thinking about ideas that belong to no single time (because they belong to all times) that education becomes a tradition and a power.

We live in a fast-food culture which manifests itself in other aspects of our lives, including reading and literature. As a culture in general, we like books that can be read quickly, often for the sake of an exciting plot or the latest bit of trendy culture. On the whole, we would almost rather do anything than read a long, meaty book. But like "fast food" for dinner, pop-culture reading is mostly unsatisfying. We consume it rapidly because there is nothing there for us to linger over, nothing to

FOREWORD

savor except temporary satiety. No one remembers a Big Mac Value Meal, and the latest "top-ten" reads are often similarly forgettable.

As a reaction against the fast-food culture, we have seen the rise of the "slow-food" movement. Slow food takes longer to prepare. Slow food pays attention to the quality of the ingredients and how well they complement each other. Slow food invests the time necessary to prepare and cook food in a way that brings out the best flavors. Slow food is never gobbled, but enjoyed at a leisurely pace, preferably in the company of others. Plutarch is slow food. Even if you could read through an entire life in one sitting, that isn't the way they are meant to be approached.

Each life is made up of incidents and occasions that are strung together, like beads on a thread, to illustrate important ideas. In cooking, one slow-food meal might showcase Italian flavors and traditions, while another slow-food meal might celebrate Korean cuisine. Plutarch allows each pair of lives in his collection to illustrate larger ideas and themes which are not confined to the life in question. Just as your single meal of delicious Italian food increases your understanding and appreciation of the Italian cuisine as a whole, reading through a single life of Plutarch increases your understanding of the ancient cultures and the universal ideas that influenced them—ideas that are still relevant for us today. That's why people—especially leaders—have never stopped reading Plutarch.

This new translation is an invitation to modern students to take a seat at the table.

As a chef would choose the best ingredients, Plutarch selected from history examples of excellence, and every generation since has sat down to enjoy the same meal. When we and our students read through these lives, we are linking ourselves into a great tradition. Either the past has something to teach us, or there is no point in studying it at all. We study the past not merely to know what happened, but to provide insight into events of today. In *A Philosophy of Education*, Charlotte Mason put her finger on this role of history: "It is never too late to mend but we may not delay to offer such a liberal and generous diet of History to every child in the country as shall give weight to his decisions, consideration to his actions and stability to his conduct." It may seem that we are asking too much of history that it have an effect on our actions today, but this is precisely why we read and study it.

As a Charlotte Mason educator, I have read a number of Plutarch's lives, but I read the life of Lycurgus for the first time in this new translation. It is no exaggeration to say that I probably enjoyed it more than I have enjoyed other readings, and for this reason, I think it will provide a bridge for students. Reading an archaic translation of Plutarch imposes distance between the student and important ideas in the text. If the student has to devote his time and attention to decoding complex sentences or archaic vocabulary, he has less time for thinking about the ideas. This readable translation brings Plutarch well within the reach of modern students who will be able to engage directly with the lawgivers for themselves.

I appreciate the efforts of Scot and David Hicks in this new translation. I hope their consideration for the expectations and capacity of modern readers will be repaid by the addition of many new learners at the feast that Plutarch has to offer. In addition to the readable text, they have included just the right amount of notes and supplementary information to bring the past into sharper focus.

Reading *Plutarch's Lives* has formed a part of the classical tradition for many centuries. As we seek to recover and rebuild that tradition of education, we must find the balance between the old and the new, the timeless and the timely. The tradition of asking the same questions that have been asked before must be continued so that the answers we find belong to our current time and circumstances. In this way classical education becomes lively and relevant to our actions today. The sixteenth-century French essayist Michael Montaigne appreciated these histories deeply and said of Plutarch: "He contents himself sometimes with only

FOREWORD

giving one brief touch to the main point of the question, and leaves the rest for us to find out for ourselves." That is what makes reading Plutarch so valuable—the opportunity to think deeply and appropriate ideas for our own use. I'm happy to know that another generation of students will be reading and thinking and discovering what Plutarch has to share.

Portrait of Plutarch, Greek historian: The caption reads: "Your wise teaching served as an impressive crown / Of Trajan, exalted above all men. / If great men heeded you[r words] in their minds and hands [to put them to practice], / Virtue would live, instead of Venus [lust] & Bellona [war]." *(Public Domain Image, Wikimedia Commons)*

An Introduction for Students New to

PLUTARCH

INTRODUCTION

I. Plutarch's Lens

It is hard for us now to appreciate how profoundly Plutarch and his writings influenced those who came after him. Shakespeare mined his *Lives* for plots; Montaigne constructed his essays along Plutarchan lines; and Rousseau claimed in his "Fourth Promenade" that Plutarch was the one writer he continued to read in old age and whose writing enriched him most. Through these writers and others, he continues to shape our understanding of the ancient world. And for that matter, it is equally hard to appreciate how utterly improbable it was that this influence should come from a gentleman farmer-teacher-priest writing in Greek and living far from Rome in a small village in the Greek countryside. Plutarch was born during the reign of the Emperor Claudius in AD 46 and lived into the time of Hadrian who ruled the Empire from AD 117 to 138. We know this because of an inscription found on a statue erected by Hadrian at Delphi, the ancient site of the oracle of Apollo, where Plutarch served for years as one of the two high priests. Delphi was a day's walk from Plutarch's home in the village of Chaeronea.

Today we remember Plutarch principally for two extended works: the *Moralia*, a selection of letters and essays compiled in the Middle Ages that gives us a wonderful insight into the intellectual concerns and world-view of someone living during the height of the Roman Empire; and the *Parallel Lives*, written over the course of a lifetime, primarily, we believe, for young people. The book you are holding in your hands contains only one of the twenty-three paired biographies—one of a Greek, the other of a Roman—contained in the surviving *Lives*. We have decided to introduce you to the *Lives* by choosing the essays on Lycurgus and Numa, although Plutarch probably wrote several of his parallel lives before these. We made this selection because it offers a rich introduction to Plutarch's Platonic way of thinking about the world he is experiencing as well as a provocative way to think about politics and religion in our own modern world. We hope these essays will whet your appetite for Plutarch and that you will want to read more of his *Lives*. Perhaps even check out the letters he writes to young friends seeking his advice in the *Moralia*.

When reading Plutarch it is important to bear a few things in mind. Like all writers, whether they do so overtly or covertly, consciously or subconsciously, Plutarch approaches his subjects from a point of view. Discerning a writer's point of view is, of course, one of the principle reasons we learn to make a close reading of texts in order to judge the reasonableness or justice of a writer's opinions and conclusions. In the case of Plutarch, you will want to do the same. To what extent is he working from reliable sources? How does his theme or thesis influence his selection of materials? Are his own political and religious views reinforced or contradicted by the stories he tells? Are the comparisons he makes apposite or forced, significant or merely obvious?

This much we can be sure of. First, Plutarch writes within the rhetorical tradition of his time, a tradition, you will remember from your studies, that Socrates criticized for being more concerned with persuasion than with truth. We observe this tradition especially at work in the genre of biography as opposed to history. With the possible exceptions of Demetrius and Antony, Plutarch chooses his biographies and their subjects as models worthy of emulation, showing the many forms that excellence can take. We may not always find these forms to our liking, but we must not make the mistake of infusing the Greek idea of excellence (*arete*) with moral content. Even thievery and tyranny can have their excellences. In the lives of Demetrius and Antony, for example, we are offered models of excellence in forms we should reject.

Plutarch makes this very point at the beginning of his life of Alexander:

As I undertake to write the life of Alexander and that of Caesar by whom Pompey was destroyed, in consideration of the vast number of deeds in question, I will in preface say only one thing: I beg my readers not to hold it against me if I have not managed to work in every single one of the famous acts reported of these men, but rather have cut most of them short. The reason is that

INTRODUCTION

> *I am writing Lives, not Histories, and the revelation of excellence or baseness does not always occur in the most conspicuous acts. Rather, some little thing, a witticism or a joke, often displays a man's character more clearly than battles with thousands of casualties, huge military formations, or sieges of cities. Just as painters carefully reproduce the face and the elements that contribute to the expression, where character is revealed, and pay very little attention to the other parts of the body, in the same way you must allow me to explore the indicators of the soul and to use these to portray each life while I leave the great accomplishments and the battles to others.* (Alexander 1)[1]

We observe here how the rhetorical tradition exercises a decisive influence on the art of biography and later, when we come to Augustine's *Confessions* and we have access to the inner life of the subject, on autobiography as well. The writer's primary interest is not the accomplishments of his subject, but the light those accomplishments and other biographical details may shed upon his subject's character. The Christians who inherited the classical tradition found this emphasis on character over accomplishment compatible with their beliefs. In a letter of St. Basil to a young man, he offers this as one of the reasons pagan authors can and should be studied in Christian schools.

Second, it will help you to understand that Plutarch is a Platonist and views the world and his subjects through a Platonic lens. If you have come to the essays on Lycurgus and Numa after having read Plato's *Republic* or the *Laws*, this will be obvious to you. If not, it may be helpful to know, for example, that Plato, having (like Thucydides) witnessed the excesses of "mob rule" in Athens during the Peloponnesian wars, favored oligarchy (rule by the few) over democracy (rule by the many). Like Plato, Plutarch believed that a philosopher's superior education and theories of government equip him to rule, or at least to advise rulers, and that a well-educated elite gov-

---

[1]. For this quotation we are using the translation found on page 71 of Robert Lamberton's *Plutarch* (Yale 2001).

erns best. Let's remember as well that the history with which Plutarch was personally acquainted seemed to support this idea. Democratic Athens condemned Socrates to death and fell first to autocratic Sparta, then to autocratic Macedonia, and finally and permanently to autocratic Rome. This was a track record America's own founding fathers had very much in mind when fashioning the "checks and balances" of their own Constitution. Our annotations throughout this translation will frequently, but by no means exhaustively, point out where Plutarch is channeling Plato.

Finally, bear in mind that Plutarch is always writing about Rome—and the Greeks and Romans—as a Greek. Although he gladly accepted Roman citizenship and the Pax Romana of his time, assuming provincial offices under Roman rule, entertaining his Roman friends at dinner parties in Chaeronea, and lecturing frequently in Rome, Plutarch is at pains to draw comparisons between Greek and Roman history that may or may not exist. His decision to write "parallel lives" is not obvious, although he makes it appear so. After all, Greece with its many and varied cities and forms of government and its rich artistic and intellectual heritage bears little resemblance to Rome with its singular and uniformly oligarchic, militaristic, expansionist, and ruthless history. Plutarch writes within a long Greek tradition beginning with Polybius that regards Greece as a sort of precursor to Rome and a civilizing influence upon the Romans. So, in the same way Virgil traces Roman lineage back to Aeneas and the Trojans, Plutarch pairs Numa with Lycurgus, the Sabines with the Spartans, and thereby suggests that Roman law and culture derived from Greeks who inhabited the plains of Lacedaemon.

II. A Brief History of the Law

In modern times we tend to think of the law as something written down and continually added to, altered, or otherwise revised by legislators in response to political and social trends and by judges who are called upon to decide between conflicting interests and expected to base their decisions on legal precedents. The fact that their interpretations of the written laws and precedents sometimes reflect their own social, political, and religious views gives rise, as we would expect, to a great deal of editorial commentary, political conflict, and social turmoil. But what we are seeing nowadays has a very long history that began with legendary lawgivers like Lycurgus and Numa. In antiquity the law was by no means understood only as that which is written down or simply for use in resolving conflicts and punishing lawlessness. A philological study (through the use of language as found in literary sources) of the development of law in ancient Greece can help us understand the complex nature and manifold uses of the law even in our own time.

Early "laws," it appears, came in three not always distinct hierarchical forms: *themistes*, *nomoi*, and *ethea*. At the top of this hierarchy were the *themistes*, the decrees handed down by the gods. Themis was the goddess of law and order, and one of the earliest divine laws in Greece was the code of hospitality to strangers (*xenia*). Both of Homer's epics turn on this unwritten code: the war on Troy in the *Iliad* resulted from Paris' violation of this code when the guest of Menelaus in Sparta, and Odysseus' slaughter of the suitors in the *Odyssey* is justified on the basis of their violation of this code in his Ithaca home. Both were cases of guests not knowing how to behave! Sophocles' tragedy *Antigone* also turns on the conflict between what he calls "the unwritten and sure ordinances of the gods" and the decree of King Creon that Antigone not be allowed to bury her brother who was killed while attacking Thebes.

In ancient Greece, the *nomoi* (written laws) were specific to each *polis* (city) and were often inscribed on the walls of the city so that visitors would be made aware of them, not unlike the posting of speed limits and fines outside towns and cities today. Solon is said to have given Athens its first *nomoi*. These were inscribed on stone in the marketplace.

Complicating this picture of the law yet further were the *ethea*: the usages, norms, and customs that governed a city, region, or people, from which our word "ethics" derives. As you will see in both Lycurgus and Numa, these customs often have their roots in religious beliefs and observances.[2] In time they can become so deeply ingrained that they form unconscious habits and require no legal enforcement. A raised eyebrow or frown (or failing these mild corrections, social ostracism) is usually all that is needed to ensure the right ethos in a traditional society. We might say that Aristotle identified virtues with these habits and defined the virtuous person as one who does the right thing spontaneously and unconsciously, without having to consider whether it is legally permissible or in his interest to act in a certain way. Upon consideration, you will appreciate how subtly and intricately these three forms of law still interact in our society and influence how we behave and experience the world around us.

The Greeks created what we now think of as schools for the purpose of instructing each rising generation of young people in these three forms of law. The Greek word for education, *paideia*, also means culture, a concept closely associated with that of the law. Schools passed on the norms of Greek culture to the future citizens of the polis, and at the same time the culture of the polis educated its citizens, as it does today—perhaps even more so through the power of modern media. In the funeral oration recorded by Thucydides, Pericles famously called Athens "an educator for all of Greece." After the conquests of Alexander the Great, the extension of Greek culture Hellenized, or made Greek, those throughout the Middle East who received this education and adopted the language and *ethea* of the Greeks.

---

[2]. For a brilliantly detailed study of this phenomenon in a modern Greek village, take a look at *Cosmos, Life, and Liturgy in a Greek Orthodox Village* (Romiosyni) by Juliet Du Boulay.

III. Law-givers Versus Law-makers

We have titled our selection of parallel lives *The Lawgivers*. It is worth reflecting on this for a moment and considering how law-givers might differ from the law-makers of the modern Western world. Our knowledge of legendary lawgivers like Hammurabi,[3] Moses, and Solon comes only in part from evidence we now consider historical, or scientifically verifiable. This is also true of Lycurgus and Numa. Much of what we claim to know about these figures derives from legends passed down through many generations or preserved in religious rituals and scriptures. There is also evidence that laws and customs emerging centuries after these figures were said or known to have lived are often attributed to them, just as they for similar reasons attributed their laws to a divine source.

Nor should we judge them harshly for making these claims. Americans, in their Declaration of Independence, asserted the claim that "all men are created equal" and "endowed by their Creator with inalienable rights." By making this claim, they attempted to base their unlawful rebellion against the English Crown on a religious belief in human equality. King George (and most of his subjects) believed he had a "divine right" to rule the colonies. Only by putting themselves on an equal footing with the King before God could the rebels make an equal claim for independence. After all, what proof is there—other than the concept of a God and Father of all mankind—that we are all equal? There is no proof—just a seemingly arbitrary assertion that must be accepted or enforced. Without this religious belief, it is hard to find evidence of human equality. Human *inequality* is what appears obvious and is, for that matter, one of the fundamental assumptions of modern science and evolutionary theory ("survival of the fittest").

---

3. Hammurabi is an interesting case. Unlike Lycurgus and Numa we have his code, but there is no legend that attaches itself to his name.

WHO WAS PLUTARCH?

The Hammurabi Stele: Hammurabi (standing) depicted as receiving his royal insignia from Shamash. Hammurabi holds his hands over his mouth as a sign of prayer (relief on the upper part of the stele of Hammurabi's code of laws).
Louvre Museum, Paris, France. Room 3: Mesopotamie, IIe millenaire avant J.-C. Richelieu, ground floor.

INTRODUCTION

We also observe in the case of lawgivers like Lycurgus and Numa that laws are "given" when societies are still not sufficiently organized or secure in their identities to "make" their own laws. Often they face a crisis created by an outside threat or an inner conflict. The purpose of the "given" law is not merely to settle the competing claims of individuals or groups, but to establish an identity and form the character of a people. Laws are "made," on the other hand, after societies are formed and the identity of a people established. They generally evolve out of competing interests, and in the modern world they are created either within the framework of a comprehensive written code as in Europe based upon the codes of Justinian and Napoleon or in the United Kingdom and United States based upon a written constitution and legal precedents like those known as Common Law.

Another feature of laws that are "given" rather than "made" may be their tendency to be regarded more positively and prescriptively (as precepts that are meant to be internalized and are necessary for the formation of a fully realized person) rather than negatively and proscriptively (as behaviors to be avoided and as limits placed upon a person's freedom). What do you think? Is the law meant primarily to prohibit and punish behaviors, or to promote and reward them? In Lycurgus' detailed instructions for raising and educating children and for all the routines of Spartan daily life, and in Numa's apparent obsession with Roman religious holidays, festivals, processions, and observances, we see evidence of a largely prescriptive interpretation of law. Because of this, you might say, Plutarch seems to be surprised by Numa's neglect of precepts for educating the young.

Moses, the famous Hebrew lawgiver with whom you are probably more familiar, offers another example of prescriptive lawgiving. He is believed by the Jews to have written the Torah, the first five books of the Bible. Although non-Jews often think of his laws as proscriptive, a matter of "thou shalt nots," they are in fact highly prescriptive and meant to form the character of the Hebrew people by defining in great detail the routines of daily life and insisting that these precepts not simply be written down, but be internalized. Moses concludes his laws by saying:

Therefore you shall lay up these words of mine in your heart and in your soul, and bind them as a sign on your hand, and they shall be immovable before your eyes. You shall teach them to your children, speaking of them when you sit in your house and walk by the way, when you lie down and rise up. You shall also write them on the doorposts of your house and your gates . . ." (Deuteronomy 11:18-20)

You will observe this insistence that the laws be taught to the young and internalized by everyone in Lycurgus and Numa as well. The culture of a people grows out of its laws, broadly understood, and the processes whereby their laws are passed on, studied, interpreted, revised, internalized, and enforced.

IV. The Historical Uses of Legend

Plutarch begins both biographies of *The Lawgivers* with an acknowledgment that his sources are few, contradictory, and perhaps more legend than history. Should this concern us? What matters most—the stories about the past that reflect a factual and true record of what actually occurred but that no one knows or believes, or the myths and legends about the past that everyone knows and most people believe? Which of these will influence how people experience the world they live in and how they see themselves and envision the future?

I think most of us would agree that our understanding of the past, whether it reflects a true or a false reality, is the lens through which we see ourselves and the world we live in. This is what makes Homer, arguably, more powerful and in that sense more real than Herodotus. It follows from this that without a universally accepted or verifiable narrative of reality, people dismiss history and turn to myth-making. This is what puts mythic figures like Lycurgus and Numa on the same footing for ancient Greeks and Romans as, say, historical figures like Jefferson

INTRODUCTION

and Napoleon are for us. Indeed, we may find less agreement amongst contemporary Americans and Frenchmen regarding the true beliefs and intentions of Jefferson and Bonaparte than existed in ancient times concerning Lycurgus and Numa amongst the Greeks and Romans.[4]

In the Preface to his history of Rome (*From the Founding of the City*, 6-7), Livy appears to answer these questions for himself. He, too, understands that his sources are suspect, but since they contain the stories that the Romans believe about themselves and their past, he makes the case that even though these stories are mythical, they are historically valid. They shaped history even if they only dimly reflected or recorded it.

> *Although our knowledge of events surrounding the founding of the city comes more from poetic tales than from the record of deeds chiseled on monuments of stone, we have no intention of affirming or denying these tales. This indulgence is granted to antiquity in order that by mixing the human and divine, the origin of cities might be regarded with greater reverence. If any people have a right to consecrate their origins and believe the gods had a hand in the founding and past glories of their city, it would have to be the Romans. Just as the world must accept the historical fact of the city's worldwide empire and clear superiority in warfare, it should also accept as fact that Mars is the father of Rome.*

Now, before dismissing this method of reasoning, we might consider how much it shares with the methods of modern science. Whether hypothesiz-

---

4. We see in this the roots of one of history's most dangerous ideas. Is "appearance tantamount to reality," as Malcolm X argued in his *Autobiography*? Was Pontius Pilate right to dismiss Christ's claim to bear witness to the truth by asking, rhetorically, "What is truth?" Is all knowledge just opinion, all history just the winner's version of what happened, or are there incontrovertible and verifiable facts and eternal verities? Plutarch and Livy appear to be identifying a "flaw" in human nature and history that might easily be exploited or lead to cynicism. In our time, this "flaw" places a premium on getting out one's version of the truth—hence propaganda, revisionist histories, ideological struggles, and the power of the media. Are we to conclude that it is not the facts that matter, but our opinions about the facts, how we see them, whether we believe them to be true or suspect that they are being presented selectively and with prejudice? Why is this a dangerous idea? How would Plutarch, as a Platonist who finds in the metaphor of the cave a picture of reality, respond to these questions?

ing a Big Bang at the moment of "creation" or assuming a human ancestry beginning with a single cell possibly delivered to Earth from some distant galaxy billions of years ago, modern scientists attempt to explain origins for which there are no known or reliable first-hand witnesses or accounts. Generally speaking, scientists offer accounts of what may have happened in the very distant past using what they observe in the present and what they know about the physical laws governing the material universe. Like Livy and all thinkers before and after him, they reason in part from what they think they know and in part from what they believe.

You will recall our caution at the beginning of this introduction about writers and their points of view. The same applies here. Just as the contemporaries of Livy's time and Livy himself assumed that there could be no adequate explanation of a beginning without divinities, modern science assumes that no account of beginnings involving a divinity is either necessary or accurate. By its nature, modern science proceeds on the assumption that everything can be understood and explained in terms of material cause and effect. For men of Livy and Plutarch's worldviews, this would rule out science as the source of a complete explanation regarding origins.

V. Judging the Past Versus Making Judgments about the Past

Finally, we have selected Lycurgus and Numa because they offer striking and sometimes shocking examples of how much our judgments concerning the ways societies ought to be organized and humans ought to behave have changed, due in no small measure to the teachings of Jesus and the influence of His Church. Although we study the past to understand and learn from it, not to judge it, we are only human and inevitably we make judgments. This is also, as we have seen, a characteristic of the rhetorical tradition of antiquity, mining the past for its life lessons and examples of human excellence. Nevertheless, there are many pitfalls in judging the past, and we should guard against the temptation to judge things prematurely—that is, to judge them, as we often do one another, before we make an effort to understand them. You may be familiar with the expression: "Don't judge another until you have walked in his or her shoes." Rushing to judgment about the past prevents us from achieving a balanced understanding of the past, from seeing things in the shades of gray they often are, and from identifying forms of excellence we might otherwise overlook.

When it comes to making judgments about the past and its people, one of the most common pitfalls involves making anachronistic judgments, e.g., judging the past by the standards of the present. For example, we read these days about college students who attack institutions that bear the names of historical figures who owned slaves, regardless of whatever else these men and women might have contributed to their societies. Certainly it is right that we should all hate the reprehensible practice of human slavery, but we know that slavery was, until modern times, a common practice throughout the world, as it still is in some places. Is it then fair to judge harshly the many men and women of the past—of all nations, races, and creeds—who practiced or tolerated slavery? As tempting as it is to make these anachronistic judgments, doing so does not change the past and only reinforces stereotypes to advance political agendas in the present. This is, of course, why it is done.

Perhaps the greatest danger in making anachronistic judgments is our failure by doing so to recognize that, like our ancestors, we, too, are caught in the web of time and profoundly, often unconsciously, influenced by the practices, views, and opinions of those around us. Had we been born in a former era, we almost certainly would have held the same views as those we criticize. How can we be so sure we would not have? It is, after all, from our own times and surroundings that we derive most of our opinions. It is also highly unlikely that some of our views today will escape the judgments of those who come after us. For this reason, our anachronistic judgments can be regarded as naive and immodest, even when they are not self-serving. And where does it end? We have no ancestors—no matter how worthy—who were not guilty of indiscretions and misdeeds, even as understood in their own time, let alone ours. Who can argue with the biblical observation that "all have sinned" (Rom. 3:23)?

This brings us to Plutarch, the great rhetorician, who offers us a form of excellence worthy of emulation, namely, an example of how to study the past without distancing ourselves from it and pretending to be superior to our subjects. In general you will find Plutarch to be sympathetic to the social, political, and religious reforms and precepts of his subjects. He is, after all, seeking to identify and celebrate those excellences in his subjects worthy of imitation. We hope you will also recognize the comparative modesty of Plutarch's claims regarding the completeness of his explanations. Not only is his modesty evident in his many disclaimers and sometimes alternative and contradictory explanations, but also in the way he qualifies his respect for his sources and subjects with humor, irony, and the occasional raised eyebrow. You will be rewarded in your search for these small gestures of his skepticism and disapproval.

Plutarch writes with great restraint. Usually he refrains from judging his subjects and their laws and practices based on his own standards of right and wrong and his own norms for acceptable behavior and political institutions. There are moments, however, when he allows himself a criticism. These moments are usually the occasion for him to question his sources or make an excuse for his subject. "We should not judge this deed too harshly," he might say, "for it was done out of necessity." Perhaps the most glaring example of this is when he describes in grisly detail the practices of the *krypteia* (the "brown shirts" or murder gangs of the Spartans). But rather than follow his sources in this matter, as he freely acknowledges, he finds a way of removing Lycurgus' responsibility for this heinous institution:

> *My own personal belief is that this cruel treatment of the helots came later than Lycurgus, especially after the great earthquake when the helots joined the Messenians in laying waste to the countryside and posing a serious threat to the city. I cannot bring myself to ascribe to Lycurgus such a bloody and barbaric institution as the krypteia, seeing elsewhere in his character and laws a consistent habit of gentleness and justice to which the gods themselves bore witness.* (Lycurgus section [28])

INTRODUCTION

How then do we judge the past in relation to the present? One way would be to compare present laws and institutions with those of antiquity. In modern times, Germany's Third Reich and the Soviet Union offer striking comparisons. But even in our own contemporary Western societies it is possible to identify social and political reforms that resemble those of Lycurgus and Numa and lay bare the pre-Christian roots of these ideas. Our judgments can then be directed, where they belong, at current practices. They can be based on outcomes rather than on a competing set of values. In this, too, we have the example of Plutarch to follow as he criticizes Numa's failure to moderate Roman avarice, pointing out the terrible excesses and injustices to which this led in the late Republic and the Empire.

A Note about the Translation

We have undertaken this translation at the request of CiRCE, the publisher. As with our earlier translation of Marcus Aurelius' so-called Meditations, *The Emperor's Handbook* (Scribner 2002), Scot starts by making a "raw" translation as close as possible to the original Greek text. Working from Scot's translation and sometimes after consulting other translations, David seeks to produce a translation that reads smoothly in English and conveys the meaning (and as much of the nuance as possible) of Plutarch's prose.

We have made what we hope is a student-friendly translation of the biographies selected by CiRCE from Plutarch's *Parallel Lives,* omitting only a couple of brief passages that seemed arcane and of little interest, but otherwise remaining entirely faithful to Plutarch's Greek text and its meaning. If you are interested, you will find our translation of the passages we omitted in the notes.

Plutarch's vocabulary is probably the richest of any of the ancient prose writers. Typically, the rules governing Greek prose were much more restrictive than those followed by the poets, but Plutarch wrote prose with the flair and freedom of a poet. This makes him difficult to translate, but fun to read. Many of our words in English have their roots in ancient Greek. We have tried to respect this fact and retain some of the Greek words in the text when we could not find a good English equivalent or when we think it's a term you may want to throw around to impress your friends.

Part of making our translation "student-friendly" was adding words and phrases to passages that allude to persons and events with which Plutarch's readers would have been familiar, but would be unfamiliar to a young reader today. In these cases, we have either offered an explanation in our notes or incorporated this information into the text itself.

Ancient Greek may be the richest and most expressive language in the world. Such a supple, flexible, nuanced language is hard to capture in what Churchill liked to call our simple, noble English tongue. Greek sentences

ABOUT THE TRANSLATION

are composed of phrases and clauses linked by particles and layered on one another in a way that continually speaks and adds to the main idea while creating a unified whole. There is in this something beautifully reflective of nature, as captured by the naturalist John Muir, who famously said, "When we try to pick out anything by itself, we find it hitched to everything else in the universe." It was easier for earlier English translators of ancient Greek to replicate this type of complex, cumulative sentence structure. For example, a translation containing the long periodic sentences constructed of dependent clauses typical of English prose during Queen Victoria's reign may come closer to the style of Plutarch, but this style is difficult and no longer pleasant for most modern readers. A modern translation, we therefore believe, will contain shorter sentences, rendering dependent clauses as independent clauses while using transitions familiar to English speakers to link these shorter sentences and produce the cumulative effect.

This is probably more than you wanted to know, but it will give you some appreciation for what's going on backstage as you enjoy the play. And enjoy the play, we hope you will.

DVH/CSH

Lycurgus as Legislator
Vorzeit und Gegenwart. *Augsbourg, 1832* M.A. Barth, Wikimedia Commons

The Life of

LYCURGUS OF SPARTA

[1] Nothing for certain can be said about Lycurgus the lawgiver. Concerning his birth, his travels, his death, even his work on the laws and constitution of Sparta, **stories differ**. Some say that he was a contemporary of Iphitus and that the two of them co-authored the **Olympic truce**. The philosopher Aristotle offers as proof of this theory a well-preserved Olympic discus on which the name of Lycurgus is engraved. Others, like **Eratosthenes and Apollodorus**, calculating from the succession of Spartan kings, judge him to be not just a few years older than the first Olympiad. Since there were two Spartans named Lycurgus who lived at different times, **Timaeus** suspects that the deeds of both were attributed to the more famous one. He believes that the older of the two lived during the time of Homer and, as some claim, may have seen him. **Xenophon** places him even earlier when he says that he lived under the Heraclids. Of course, by birth the most recent Spartan kings are Heraclids, but Xenophon probably means that Lycurgus lived close to the time of Heracles himself. Whatever the case and in spite of these inconsistencies, we shall try to tell the story of the man's life by using the least contested details and following the most respected written **accounts**.

[2] The most admired of Lycurgus' ancestors is Soos under whom the Spartans made slaves of the helots and annexed much of the country belonging to the Arcadians. It is said that when Soos was besieged by the Cleitorians in a wilderness without water, he agreed to abandon the territory he had taken if he and all his men were allowed to drink from a nearby spring. Having sworn oaths of agreement, he gathered his men and promised that he would give the kingship to anyone who refused to drink. But none had the strength to refuse. All drank. After they had drunk, **Soos** (without drinking) bathed in the spring while the enemy looked on, and he ended up keeping the territory inasmuch as not everyone had drunk.

Even though the Spartans admired him for these acts of courage, they named his family the Eurypontids after his son Eurypon, who was the first to relax the strict monarchy in an effort to win over and please the people.

NOTES

Stories differ: A remarkably succinct and accurate statement of exactly where we stand today.

Olympic truce: A truce for the period of the Olympic Games was instituted at the first Olympiad in 776 BC. Plutarch would probably have found Aristotle's mention of the inscription in his *Constitution of Sparta*.

Eratosthenes and Apollodorus: Eratosthenes (third century BC), sometimes referred to as the Father of Geography, was a scholar and chief librarian at Alexandria. He is famous for having calculated the circumference of the earth and the tilt of its axis, both with remarkable accuracy. He established a chronology, which was followed by Apollodorus, also a librarian at Alexandria who eventually moved to the rival library at Pergamum.

Timaeus: Of Locri, who gives his name to Plato's dialogue.

Xenophon: In his *Constitution of Sparta* 10.8. Cf. Herodotus I.65.4 where he is the guardian of Leobotus, seven generations from Heracles. According to Herodotus' dating of Heracles (II.145) and his method of calculating generations, that puts Lycurgus in the eleventh century BC. Plutarch does not follow Herodotus, however, and in the passage that follows (see note on Accounts below), he seems to follow the "majority" (*hoi pleistoi*) in placing him eleven generations from Heracles, so in the tenth or ninth century BC. Modern scholarship dates his reforms to "the half-century or so around 650" (Forrest 58).

Accounts: Detailing the differing accounts of Lycurgus' ancestry is left out of our translation. The missing passage reads as follows: "Although the poet Simonides says that Lycurgus was not the son of Eunomos but that Lycurgus and Eunomos were sons of Prytanis, most writers give a very different genealogy. They say that Procles, son of Aristodemos, engendered Soos, that Soos engendered Eurypon, Eurypon Prytanis, and Prytanis Eunomos. They say that from Eunomos and a first wife, Polydectes was born, and that from his second wife named Dionasse, Lycurgus was born. And so the historian Dieutychidas puts him six generations from Procles and eleven from Heracles."

Soos: Soos does not appear in the list of Spartan kings and does not figure in Herodotus' account. The story of his having tricked the Arcadians is similar to many stories from the period of Greek colonization, where the native population is tricked out of territory by the wording of an agreement.

As a consequence of this leniency, the people grew bold, and their kings were either hated for using force against them, or yielded to them out of weakness or to win their favor. And so, lawlessness and disorder reigned in Sparta for a long period. It was during this time that the father of Lycurgus was king and fell victim to lawlessness, struck by a kitchen knife while trying to break up a fight, and leaving the kingship to his eldest son Polydectes.

[3] When Polydectes died a short time later, everyone thought Lycurgus should be king. He did in fact reign, but only until it became evident that **his brother's wife** was pregnant. As soon as he noticed this, he announced that the kingdom belonged to her child, if a male, and he would rule only as the boy's guardian. (The Spartans call the guardians of orphan kings *prodikoi*—upholders of rights.) The woman, however, sent him a secret message saying that she would destroy the child in her womb if as king of Sparta he would promise to marry her. Lycurgus loathed the woman's wickedness, but rather than reject her offer, he pretended to welcome it. He merely cautioned her not to ruin her health and risk her life by taking drugs to abort the fetus. Instead, he promised to get rid of the child himself as soon as it was born. In this way he led the widow on throughout her pregnancy. When word came to him that she was in labor, he sent servants to assist the midwives and gave them strict instructions that if the child was a girl, she was to be handed over to the women, and if it was a boy, he was to be brought to him immediately, wherever he was, whatever he was doing. It so happened that he was dining with the magistrates when his servants arrived bearing a baby boy. It is said that he took the babe in his arms and announced to everyone present, "Spartans, unto you a king is born!" He then laid the babe down in the king's place and gave him the name of Charilaos (the joy of his people) because everyone was overjoyed as well as deeply impressed with Lycurgus' wisdom and justice.

Although Lycurgus had reigned for a total of only eight months, the citizens of Sparta all admired him. They eagerly desired to do whatever

NOTES

[3]: This entire chapter merits comparison to Plato's description of the Philosopher-King, especially to the conclusion of the Allegory of the Cave (*Republic* 519b ff.).

His brother's wife: The only aspect of this story that falls outside the ancient norms is Lycurgus' assumption of the paternal role in volunteering to expose the newborn, but even there his assumption of responsibility for his widowed sister-in-law would be considered normal and proper in many ancient societies. Lycurgus' objection to her behavior is rather based on the fact that her child, if male, should be the future king. In his discussion of marriage and child-bearing for example, Aristotle, whose discussion in *Politics* vii.16 sets limits on the use of late abortion, recommends a law to require exposure of deformed children and another to set limits on the number of children if local law prohibits exposure and to require an early abortion if that number is exceeded. In general, Greco-Roman law regarded a child as the property of its father, who at birth would either accept the child into the household or leave it to be exposed or sold. By Plutarch's day, low birth rates had long reached crisis proportions among the Greco-Roman upper classes owing to inheritance laws and the desire to maintain one's estate. The emperor Augustus attempted to address the problem, and eventually the emperors Septimius Severus and Caracalla issued bans on abortion. There is evidence of moral repugnance at abortion techniques in pagan society, but the moral revolution in Western thought is owing to the advent of Christianity, which early on, in *The Teachings of the Apostles, Letter of Barnabas,* and the early Church Fathers, Clement of Alexandria and Tertullian, condemned the practice as homicide.

he asked of them less on account of his authority as guardian of the child king than out of their admiration for his character. Of course, there were also those who envied and hated him and tried to stand in the way of his advancement as a young man. In particular this group included the relatives and household of the king's mother, who considered herself disrespected. Her brother, Leonidas, once insulted Lycurgus to his face by insinuating that he was aware of Lycurgus' plan to someday become king. This naturally gave rise to suspicions and made it likely that if anything were to happen to the child king, Lycurgus would be blamed for having planned it. The queen mother and her friends spread similar rumors. Troubled by all this and fearing where it might lead, Lycurgus decided to escape suspicion by going abroad and traveling from place to place until his nephew was old enough to father a child and legitimate **heir to the throne**.

[4] He first went to Crete. There he studied the island's various forms of government and spoke with the most reputable men. Some of their laws he admired and borrowed for use at home; others he found useless. By making friends through acts of kindness with the Cretan most highly regarded for his learning and political wisdom, Lycurgus persuaded him to go to Sparta. This man, Thales by name, built his reputation as a **lyric poet**. This skill he used to embellish and advance his brilliant ideas as a lawgiver. The soothing music and gentle cadence of his odes, telling tales celebrating obedience and concord, imperceptibly softened the behavior of his listeners and led them to put aside the private feuding and mutual hostilities that were then common and to live together in pursuit of the common good. It is fair to say that in this way he laid the groundwork for the reforms Lycurgus would later introduce to Sparta.

From Crete he sailed to Asia. There, like a doctor who compares healthy bodies with wounded and diseased ones, we are told that Lycurgus intended to compare the Cretan way of life and form of government, so simple and severe, to that of the Ionians, so extravagant and permissive. There he

NOTES

Heir to the throne: This aspect of Lycurgus' "personal" story may strike us as the most suspect. What happened to his trusteeship? And of course his travels just happen to be a repeat of Menelaus'—legendary king of Sparta—and anticipate Solon the Lawgiver's better documented ones.

Lyric poet: Early Greek philosophical and "scientific" texts were generally written in verse in a genre we now label didactic. See for example Hesiod's *Works and Days* or Parmenides' *On Nature*. For an explicit lawgiver-poet parallel see Solon the Lawgiver's poetry.

also encountered for the first time the poetry of Homer, preserved, possibly, by the **descendants of Creophilus**. Recognizing that the political wisdom and educational merit in this poetry more than compensates for the **bad behavior it sometimes seems to celebrate**, he eagerly made copies of the poems with the intention of using them back home in Sparta. At this time few Greeks were familiar with Homer, and those who were only knew his poetry from short passages plucked at random from his works. **It was Lycurgus who made Homer's poetry famous**.

The Egyptians also claim that Lycurgus visited them. Being especially impressed by their manner of separating a warrior class from the rest of society, he adopted this practice for Sparta. By **allowing artisans and manual laborers no role in government**, he expected to lend refinement and beauty to the state. Some Greek writers confirm this Egyptian account. On the other hand, claims that he visited Africa and Spain, and spoke with the **Gymnosophists** on a voyage to India, come from only one source, so far as we know: **Aristocrates** the Spartan, son of Hipparchus.

[5] The Spartans missed Lycurgus in his absence and often sent for him. "We have plenty of those who bear the title and wear the privileges of kings," they said, "but their abilities make them no more deserving of these honors than the rest of us." Only in Lycurgus did they see the qualities of a natural leader and the ability to inspire others to follow him. Nor did the kings oppose his return. Indeed, they hoped that with him at their side the Spartans would show them more respect.

Finding everyone in this frame of mind when he returned home, Lycurgus resolved to shake things up and rewrite the entire constitution on the theory that piecemeal or incremental change would not remedy what ailed Sparta any more than changing dosages of the same drugs and purges will heal a patient who suffers from multiple illnesses. The patient needs a whole new treatment! With this in mind he left for Delphi to consult the god there. After making the obligatory sacrifices, he received from Pythian Apollo the now famous oracle stating that he was "beloved

NOTES

Descendants of Creophilus: A slight indication perhaps that the standard modern dates for Lycurgus are on target.

Bad behavior it sometimes seems to celebrate: A passage which recalls Plato's readings of Homer in the *Republic* and the *Ion*. As striking examples of both in Homer, the Phaeacian minstrel's story in the *Odyssey* 8 and the depiction of the homicide trial on the shield of Achilles in the *Iliad* 18 might be cited. In the former, the bandy-legged blacksmith god Hephaestus crafts an invisible net to catch his wife, the lovely Aphrodite, in bed with macho-man Ares and angrily invites all the other gods to come and watch. The goddesses stay home for shame, but all the gods come and can't help bursting into laughter at what is indeed a fine roasting of all three divinities. The entire passage inevitably came up for axing by some critics. In the latter, a call for the blood-price (a death for a death) by the family of the victim is overcome by a trial before the city elders sitting in a "sacred circle" and with a prize for the judge who spoke "the straightest verdict"—nothing less than a proud declaration of civilization's hard-won victory over tribalism.

It was Lycurgus who made Homer's poetry famous: Plutarch might have found this account in the works of the minor fourth-century BC historian Ephorus. While it could always be true, the well-known association of the Homeric texts with Peisistratus of Athens makes it a likely result of anti-Athenian propaganda.

Allowing artisans and manual laborers no role in government: Plato's *Republic* again.

Gymnosophists: Naked teachers, the Greek term for the Brahmans.

Aristocrates: Are we getting a glimpse of Plutarch's sense of humor?

of the gods, more god than man, and since he sought **good governance**, would be given by far the strongest and best of all **constitutions**."

Encouraged by the god's words, Lycurgus approached Sparta's leading citizens and asked them to help him make the changes he envisioned. (Hermippus recorded the names of the twenty most prominent men who sided with Lycurgus, but the one closest to Lycurgus and most instrumental in helping to frame and implement the new laws was Arthmiadas.) He first spoke privately with his friends and gradually enlarged this circle until he had enough supporters to act. When this moment came, he ordered thirty of the leading citizens to arm themselves and meet him at dawn in the marketplace. This, he reckoned, would strike terror into the hearts of those who opposed him.

When the tumult that followed broke out, King Charilaos, fearing that the whole affair was directed against him, fled to the **House of Bronze** for sanctuary. Later, being a gentle soul by nature and after receiving sworn guarantees of his safety, he left his sanctuary and took part in the unfolding events. This story is confirmed by the remark of his fellow king Archelaus who, upon once hearing the young man being praised, said, "How can you call Charilaos anything but good? He's good even to the bad."

The first and greatest of Lycurgus' many innovations was the establishment of a **senate of elders**. **As Plato says**, by making the senate's voice equal to the king's on the really important questions, the government ensured the health of the state and protected it against the capricious exercise of royal power. Like a ship's ballast, the senate steadied the state, placing it on an **even keel**. Otherwise, the state tended to lurch between the extremes of tyranny with the kings and democracy with the people. Instead, the twenty-eight senators kept the state safe by supporting the kings when they sensed the state slipping into democracy and siding with the people when the kings started acting like tyrants.

Why twenty-eight? Aristotle says that of the thirty originally chosen by Lycurgus, two for want of courage backed out. **Sphaerus**, however, assures us that there were twenty-eight senators from the beginning. It could

NOTES

Good governance: The Greek term *eunomia*, which we have translated as "good governance," became a catchword in this era of lawmaking in archaic Greece. It was used by the Spartan poet Tyrtaeus in the late seventh century BC and was the title of a panegyric poem by Solon, the lawgiver of Athens. We might compare the use of "utopia" as a catchword of the European Renaissance.

Constitutions: The Greek word *politeia*, which we generally translate as "constitution," is used as the title of Plato's famed dialogue translated as the *Republic*. It is a broad term used to designate the form a society (or *polis*) takes. It does not designate a written document as in the US constitution but rather the form of society envisioned by the Founding Fathers.

House of Bronze: The *Chalkioikos*, or House of Bronze, was the name given to the temple of Athena on the Spartan acropolis.

Senate of elders: In Greek, literally, the old men (*gerontes*) who formed the Greek *Gerousia*, Latin *Senate* (again from *senes*, old men). Still make sense?

As Plato says: In the *Laws* 691e-692a, including the medical metaphor.

Even keel: Plato employs the metaphor of a stay used to prop up a ship on shore.

Sphaerus: Sphaerus was a disciple of Zeno (founder of the *Stoa*) who probably introduced Stoicism to Sparta, where he was an advisor to Cleomenes III. Among his many works (now lost) was one on the Spartan Constitution and three books on Lycurgus and Socrates.

also be because twenty-eight is achieved by multiplying **seven times four**, making it the first of the perfect numbers after six that is also equal to the **sum of its factors**. Personally, I think Lycurgus chose the number twenty-eight so that there would be **thirty** once the two kings were added.

[6] Lycurgus attached so much importance to this form of government that he brought back from Delphi an oracle about it called a **rhetra**. It reads as follows:

> *Build a temple to Zeus Skyllanios and Athena Skyllania, divide the people into tribes and* obai, *appoint a senate of thirty men including the chief magistrates, and celebrate the Feast of Apollo from time to time between the* Babyka *and the* Knakion. *At this time issues can be raised and proposals made, but the people in assembly will have the final say.*

This text instructs Lycurgus to divide the people into groups and subgroups called tribes and *obai*. The chief magistrates are the kings. And to celebrate the Feast of Apollo, whom Lycurgus believed to be **the source of his constitution**, means to hold an assembly. The *Babyka* is now called <text missing> and the *Knakion* the *Oenous*. Aristotle says the *Babyka* is a bridge and the *Knakion* a river. The Spartans held their assemblies between them even though there were no council chambers or other buildings there. Lycurgus felt that these added nothing to a deliberative process and were in fact hindrances to sound decision-making. With their statues and inscriptions, theatrical embellishments and **fine-fretted ceilings**, they merely distracted those present from the business at hand and filled their heads with all sorts of silly and vainglorious thoughts. When the citizens gathered there in the open air, none was allowed to question or voice an opinion; they were present simply to accept or reject whatever the kings and senators proposed. Later, however, when the citizens managed to distort or place restrictions on proposals by adding a phrase here or deleting a word there, the kings **Polydorus and Theopompus** amended the Rhetra to read:

NOTES

Seven times four: Seven being the perfect number. Four original villages seem to have incorporated to make up Sparta, but otherwise the number does not appear to be an organizing factor in the Spartan constitution.

Sum of its factors: 1+2+3=6; 1+2+3+4+7+14=28

Thirty: Why Plutarch regards thirty as a magic number he doesn't say. Presumably not because it was also the number of the puppet government known as the Thirty Tyrants set up in Athens by Sparta after her defeat in the Second Peloponnesian War.

Rhetra: A *rhetra* is in Homer, and in general use later, a verbal agreement or covenant, and the word is found in an archaic (sixth-century BC) inscription in the Doric and Elean dialects to refer to a treaty. As Plutarch tells us later (section [13]), the Spartans called Lycurgus' laws *rhetrai*, and one of these stipulated that none should be written down. Presumably then, the Spartans refer to this Delphic oracle as a rhetra (or Great Rhetra as it is sometimes called) by extension because it is the divine consecration of the central pillar of the Lycurgan legislation. Whatever the case may be, inasmuch as the Delphic oracles were recorded, it is the one piece of hard historical evidence we have for the Lycurgan reforms, just as the oracle alluded to in section [5] (and also found in Herodotus I.65) is the best proof we have of Lycurgus himself.

The source of his constitution: Lycurgus' use of the Delphic oracle and attribution of credit to Apollo for his legislation are consistent with other early lawgivers, starting with the earliest complete code of which we have a copy preserved, dated circa 1750 BC, that of Hammurabi, king of Babylon, and including the foundation of the Judeo-Christian legal tradition in the account of Moses and the Ten Commandments (Ex. 19-20). See excerpt below.

Fine-fretted ceilings: Plutarch likely has Athens, the usual target, in mind again, where the assembly sometimes met in the Theater of Dionysus.

Polydorus and Theopompus: The approximate dates of their reigns are in the early seventh century, a date that coincides with our modern approximate dates for Lycurgus. It remains a question on whose authority Plutarch calls this part of the rhetra a later addition. If he found the rhetra in Aristotle's lost *Constitution of the Lacedaemonians*, as is commonly believed, it is by no means necessary that he is following Aristotle's judgment here, and it is likely that the rhetra itself contained this "article" without comment. The most authoritative modern account conjectures that Lycurgus acted under the aegis of Polydorus (Forrest 65-68).

> *If the citizens twist the meaning of the original proposals, the senators and chief magistrates (the two kings) may lawfully dissolve the assembly.*

In other words, if the citizens have altered or distorted the original proposals in a manner not serving the best interest of Sparta, the leaders may withdraw their proposals and dissolve the assembly. Polydorus and Theopompus even managed to convince the people that Apollo Himself ordered this change to the Rhetra, as **these words** as these words by the poet Tyrtaeus seem to suggest:

> *In obedience to Phoebus, from Pytho home they bore*
> *oracles of the god, infallible words:*
> *the god-favored kings, protectors of lovely Sparta,*
> *carry the most weight in council,*
> *along with the reverend senators, then men of the citizenry,*
> *obeying in turn the straight rhetrae.*

[7] Lycurgus **mixed his constitution** in this way. But in spite of this, those who followed him found the oligarchical element in the government still too strong. To control this element and check its high spirits, as Plato wrote in **the Laws**, they put a bridle called the ephorate in its mouth. Elatus and his fellow ephors were appointed about 130 years after Lycurgus, **when Theopompus was king**. They say his wife chided him for leaving the kingship to his children smaller than he had received it from his ancestors. "No," he replied, "greater, because it will last longer." Indeed, by placing reasonable limits on their authority, the Spartan kings escaped the jealousies that undid the Argive and Messinian kings who were unwilling to share or relax their authority in the direction of the people.

The wisdom and foresight of Lycurgus is nowhere seen more clearly than when we consider the misgovernment and feuding between the citizens and kings of Sparta's near neighbors and fellow Dorians, the Argives and Messinians. In the beginning all these states were dealt pretty much the same hand.

NOTES

These words: His elegiac *Eunomia*. See the note about this type of poetry on page 27.

Mixed his constitution: The notion of a mixed constitution, one that provides checks and balances among its different elements, was a favored notion in classical Greek political thought and gained added authority later when the historian Polybius applied it (mistakenly, it turns out) to the Roman Republic. This becomes one of the reasons that the Romans will be said to have borrowed their constitution from the Spartans. See "The Life of Numa."

The *Laws*: In the *Laws* 692a. Putarch quotes Plato almost verbatim.

When Theopompus was king: At this point, Plutarch is following Eratosthenes' chronology that dated the institution of the ephorate to 755 BC.

THE CODE OF HAMMURABI
(EXCERPTS)

When Anu the Sublime, King of the Anunaki, and Bel, the lord of Heaven and earth, who decreed the fate of the land, assigned to Marduk, the over-ruling son of Ea, God of righteousness, dominion over earthly man, and made him great among the Igigi, they called Babylon by his illustrious name, made it great on earth, and founded an everlasting kingdom in it, whose foundations are laid so solidly as those of heaven and earth; then Anu and Bel called by name me, Hammurabi, the exalted prince, who feared God, to bring about the rule of righteousness in the land, to destroy the wicked and the evil-doers; so that the strong should not harm the weak; so that I should rule over the black-headed people like Shamash, and enlighten the land, to further the well-being of mankind.

That the strong might not injure the weak, in order to protect the widows and orphans, I have in Babylon the city where Anu and Bel raise high their head, in E-Sagil, the Temple, whose foundations stand firm as heaven and earth, in order to bespeak justice in the land, to settle all disputes, and heal all injuries, set up these my precious words, written upon my memorial stone, before the image of me, as king of righteousness.

EPILOGUE

LAWS of justice which Hammurabi, the wise king, established. A righteous law, and pious statute did he teach the land. Hammurabi, the protecting king am I. I have not withdrawn myself from the men, whom Bel gave to me, the rule over whom Marduk gave to me, I was not negligent, but I made them a peaceful abiding-place. I expounded all great difficulties, I made the light shine upon them.

(Continued on page 37)

If anything the territorial advantage went to the Argives and Messinians. But their good fortune did not last long. The arrogance of their kings and the unruliness of their citizens threw everything into confusion and undermined the established order and institutions. Were the Spartans not truly blessed by the gods to have a man like Lycurgus to bring **balance** to their government and harmony to their society? **More on this later** . . .

[8] The second and most audacious of Lycurgus' reforms was the **redistribution of land**. There was terrible inequality throughout Laconia, and wealth was concentrated in only a few hands. Those without property or any means of supporting themselves crowded into the city. To end this and rid the state of arrogance and jealousy, vice and luxury, and all the other social ills attending extremes of wealth and poverty, Lycurgus urged upon the Spartans a complete redistribution of all their land. All would live together as equals with equal shares of property on which to earn their livelihoods. The measure of a citizen's virtue would be the only mark of superiority since there is no real difference from one man to the next except in his behavior, whether deserving of blame for being base or worthy of praise for being noble.

True to his word, he distributed Laconia in thirty thousand lots to those living in the country, and nine thousand lots to the **Spartiates** who paid tribute and lived in the city. Some say that Lycurgus distributed six thousand lots to the city-dwellers and that Polydorus added three thousand later. Others say they each distributed four thousand. The size of each lot was meant to produce seventy **medimni** of barley for the man and twelve for his wife along with a proportionate amount of fruit and vegetables. Lycurgus believed that this amount of food would be enough to keep the owners fit and healthy without needing anything more. It is said that later in life, returning from a trip abroad at harvest time, he observed the equal stacks of grain piled neatly on the side of the road and commented to those traveling with him, "All Laconia looks like a large family farm recently inherited by many brothers."

NOTES

(Continued from page 35.)

> The king who ruleth among the kings of the cities am I. My words are well considered; there is no wisdom like unto mine. By the command of Shamash, the great judge of heaven and earth, let righteousness go forth in the land: by the order of Marduk, my lord, let no destruction befall my monument. In E-Sagil, which I love, let my name be ever repeated; let the oppressed, who has a case at law, come and stand before this my image as king of righteousness; let him read the inscription, and understand my precious words: the inscription will explain his case to him; he will find out what is just, and his heart will be glad, so that he will say:
>
> "Hammurabi is a ruler, who is as a father to his subjects, who holds the words of Marduk in reverence, who has achieved conquest for Marduk over the north and south, who rejoices the heart of Marduk, his lord, who has bestowed benefits for ever and ever on his subjects, and has established order in the land."
>
> In future time, through all coming generations, let the king, who may be in the land, observe the words of righteousness which I have written on my monument; let him not alter the law of the land which I have given, the edicts which I have enacted; my monument let him not mar. If such a ruler have wisdom, and be able to keep his land in order, he shall observe the words which I have written in this inscription; the rule, statute, and law of the land which I have given; the decisions which I have made will this inscription show him; let him rule his subjects accordingly, speak justice to them, give right decisions, root out the miscreants and criminals from this land, and grant prosperity to his subjects.
>
> *Translated by L. W. King. Ancient History Encyclopedia (ancient.eu).*

Balance: Plutarch comes back to the notion of a mixed constitution in his conclusion.

More on this later: See sections [28] and [29] below.

Redistribution of land: From a modern perspective, this reform could be seen as the basis for the entire Lycurgan system, and this section gives us some of the best information we have, as uncertain as it seems, on the size and growth of Sparta.

Spartiates: Also the "Equals," designate full male citizens. Those who maintained their status were admitted to the assembly at age thirty, but the designation and lot attached to it was determined at birth (Forrest 52).

Medimni: A *medimnus* was the equivalent of roughly one and a half bushels US.

[9] Next he attempted a redistribution of furniture, hoping in this way to remove entirely any signs of inequality and ranking by wealth. But when he saw that the citizens refused to accept downright confiscation of their personal possessions, he decided to attack their avarice by political means. He invalidated the use of gold and silver **coinage** and made iron the only legal tender. Moreover, he assigned such a small value to a great weight of iron that it would take a large room to store **ten minae's worth** and a team of oxen just to haul it around. The spread of this currency drove many types of crime from Lacedaemon. Who would ever want to steal or use as a bribe something he could not hide, did not particularly want to possess, and could not break up and put to another use? They say that when the iron was red-hot and being hammered out, Lycurgus ordered that it be tempered in vinegar, thereby making it brittle and almost unworkable for other uses.

After this he outlawed any useless **crafts** or luxury professions. Even if he had not done so, they would probably have died a natural death since the market for their services inevitably dried up. No one wanted to be paid in iron, and it could not be used to make even simple purchases from other Greeks, who made fun of it and refused to trade with Sparta and accept payment in iron. Without a currency valued by outsiders, Laconia was no longer visited by itinerant teachers, huckstering fortunetellers, pimps, and makers of gold and silver jewelry. Deprived in this way of the things luxury feeds on, luxury itself little by little wasted away. There being no public outlet or market for their wealth, the rich lost all advantage over the poor, and their wealth had to stay indoors, so to speak. This explains why essential household utensils and furniture in Sparta—beds, chairs, and tables—are so finely crafted. Consider, for example, the Spartan army drinking mug that, according to **Critias**, is particularly prized. Its color hides the nasty appearance of the water soldiers are obliged to drink, and its rim catches and holds the muddy sediments inside and allows only the clean water to reach the drinker's mouth. The lawgiver **deserves** credit for this as well. No longer having to make useless trash, craftsmen could now apply their talents to more essential work.

NOTES

Coinage: This appears to be one of the "Lycurgan" reforms accredited to him at a later date. The earliest gold and silver coinage in the Greek world was issued in Asia in the late seventh century BC and the earliest coinage minted on the Greek mainland dates to the mid-sixth century. An earlier form of utensil-money, however, was used in the Greek world in the form of long spits (used in sacrifice) made of bronze or copper called *obols*, which were traded in handfuls (Greek *drachmae*) of six, that gave their names to Greek coins ancient and modern. Apparently, the Spartans continued to use this form of currency in the form of heavier iron *obols* for internal trading purposes.

Ten minae's worth: A mina of silver was worth one hundred drachmas. In the classical period, a drachma was considered a day's wage.

Crafts: This item provides us with a way to compare the archaeological evidence, which points to flourishing decorative arts in Sparta until a dramatic decline in the mid-sixth century (i.e., well after a reasonable date for Lycurgus and suggesting another later reform accredited to the legendary lawgiver).

Critias: The leader of the Thirty Tyrants imposed on Athens after their defeat in the Second Peloponnesian War who wrote a treatise on the Spartan constitution.

Deserves: The Greek clause needs no verb, allowing Plutarch to continue to describe the work of Lycurgus in the past while making a general statement about legislators.

[10] To further restrict luxury and remove the desire for wealth, Lycurgus introduced his third and most beautiful reform: **the common meal**. He proposed that the people come together to eat in common from **a simple fixed menu**. No longer were they to eat at home reclining at table on ornate couches, waited on in shady nooks by fancy cooks and pastry chefs, fattening themselves like brute beasts, and ruining not only their bodies but also their morals by indulging every desire to the point of wanting long naps, hot baths, extended leisure, and the pampering usually prescribed for the sick. This was quite an achievement, but even greater than making wealth unenviable was making it undesirable by robbing it of its very attributes. As long as the rich man sat down at the same table as the poor man, no longer could he enjoy or take pride in the display of his riches. This is why the Greeks say that in all the world only in Sparta does **Ploutos**, the god of wealth, hang like a painting on the wall—blind, lifeless, and still. Nor was it allowed to eat beforehand and go to the common meal with a full stomach. Everyone was wise to this trick and quick to ridicule as weak or dainty anyone who failed to eat and drink the common fare.

[11] This last reform, it is said, especially exasperated the wealthy citizens of Sparta. They ganged up on Lycurgus in the marketplace, shouting their discontent and throwing stones and forcing him to flee for his life and seek sanctuary in the temple. He managed to outrun all of his pursuers except one, a young man named Alcander, who was otherwise a decent fellow but on this occasion simply excited and worked up. When Alcander caught up, Lycurgus turned toward him, and without thinking Alcander struck the lawgiver with his staff and put out one of his eyes. Undaunted, Lycurgus stood his ground and showed the citizens pursuing him his bloodied face and smashed eye. So great was their shame and remorse at this sight that they handed Alcander over to him for punishment and led him back to the home of Lycurgus, all the time expressing their regret.

After thanking them for their concern, Lycurgus sent everyone except Alcander away and led the young man into his house without harming

NOTES

The common meal: The Spartan *sussitia*.

A simple fixed menu: Plutarch seems to be referring to the Spartan staples of barley bread and a black broth made of meat, blood, vinegar, and salt.

Ploutos: Aristophanes' Ploutos in his play by that name provides a good explanation of his blindness when he says (*Plutus* 87-92):

> *Zeus made me this way out of jealousy for mankind.*
> *When I was still a lad I threatened to visit*
> *Only the just, the wise, and the well behaved.*
> *He made me blind so I couldn't tell men apart.*
> *That's how jealous he is of worthy men.*

him in any way or uttering a word of blame. He merely dismissed his usual servants and caregivers and ordered Alcander to wait on him. Being honorable, Alcander did whatever he was told without complaining. He ended up staying and living with Lycurgus, experiencing firsthand his kindness, his high-mindedness, his ascetical lifestyle, and his indefatigable work ethic. Having grown from uninformed enemy to informed admirer, he told all his family and friends that Lycurgus was not the arrogant and surly man he had once imagined him to be, but the kindest and gentlest soul in all the world. So this was Alcander's punishment: He had to change from being a willful and undisciplined youth to become one of Sparta's most well-mannered and wise citizens.

In memory of what he had suffered, Lycurgus built a temple to Athena that he named *Optillete* because the Dorians call the eyes *optills*. Some writers, however, among them Dioscorides who wrote a treatise on the Spartan constitution, claim that Lycurgus' eye was struck but not blinded by the blow, and that he built the sanctuary to the goddess as a thank offering for his healing. Whatever the case, after this misadventure the Spartans no longer carried staves into their assemblies.

[12] The Spartans gather for their common meals in a **cohort** of roughly fifteen members. Every month each member brings a bushel of barley, eight gallons of wine, five pounds of cheese, two and a half pounds of figs, and a little money for condiments. Other than this requirement, when anyone makes a sacrifice to the gods or is out late hunting and cannot attend the common meal, he is expected to send a portion of his sacrifice or kill to the cohort since on these occasions he is allowed to eat at home. This custom of the common meal was enforced for a long time. In this regard, consider the fate of King Agis who, returning to Sparta after having just defeated the Athenians in battle, wished to dine at home with his wife. He sent for his portion of the meal, but the generals refused to send it. And when the next day, still smarting from their refusal, he neglected to make the obligatory thanksgiving offering to the gods, the generals fined him.

NOTES

Cohort: We have omitted Plutarch's two sentences that offer competing etymologies for the Spartan word for cohort, *phiditia*. These sentences read as follows: Common meals are called *andreia* by the Cretans and *phiditia* by the Spartans, either because they provided for friendship and affection, substituting a delta (*phiditia*) for the lambda in *philitia*, or because they encourage economy and parsimony (*pheido*). But nothing prevents an initial letter (*phi*) from having been added, as some say, to *editia* to mean diet and food (*edode*).

Children also attended the common meal as part of their education in self-discipline. This is where they heard political discussions and observed the pleasant give and take of free men often tinged with humor. Here they gained the habit of teasing without delivering insults and of being teased without taking offense. This is very much a Spartan trait and sign of good breeding: the ability to take a joke. By the same token, if the person on the receiving end of the joke was in any way offended, he could protest and the joking would stop forthwith. The senior member of the cohort greeted everyone at the doors of the common meal with the words, "Nothing said here leaves this room."

The person hoping to join a cohort is tested as follows: The members each take a chunk of bread in their hand, and as a servant circles the room with a basket on his head, they toss their chunks into the basket. If they approve the candidate, they leave their chunks unchanged; those who do not approve close their fist around the chunk and crush it. The crushed chunk means the same as a pierced voting disc. If even one crushed chunk is found in the basket, the candidate is rejected, since it is important for everyone to enjoy each member's company. They say that a rejected candidate has been *caddized*, a term derived from the name of the basket (*caddichos*) into which they cast their "bread ballots."

Their favorite dish is their famous black broth, so much so that the older members leave whatever morsels of meat they receive for the younger men and eat only the broth. There is a story that one of the kings of Pontus, having heard so much about this famous broth, asked a Spartan cook to prepare it for him. When the king found the taste of it disgusting, the cook excused himself by saying, "Your majesty, only those who have washed in the river Eurotas can stomach this broth."

Finally, regarding the custom of the common meal, the members of each cohort drink only in moderation and leave the meal without carrying a torch. In fact, on no occasion are Spartans allowed to light their way at night with torches so that they become accustomed to traveling boldly and fearlessly in the darkness of night.

Roman Terracotta Bowl
This ancient Roman bowl may have been a part of the types of meals described. It shows traces of a decorative green glaze on reddish terracotta.
Metropolitan Museum of Art, NY. (Public Domain Image)

[13] Lycurgus never wrote down his laws. In fact, one of his so-called rhetras expressly forbade written law. Rather, he believed that the best lawgiver is education, particularly an education that implants in every young person a firm resolve to act within the spirit of the law and the **lawgiver's intentions**. This works better than any form of constraint to secure the happiness and protection of the state. Regarding more minor matters like business contracts that are always changing as circumstances change, he thought it best not to prescribe fixed rules or customs, but to let these matters be resolved by the **competent** authorities as they arise. Everything depended not on law, but on education, and for that reason one of his rhetras opposed the writing of laws.

Another rhetra, yet another against luxury, stipulated that no other tools besides an axe for the rafters and a saw for the doors be used in the construction of a Spartan house. By assuming that such a house left no room for luxury or extravagance, Epaminondas was probably taking a leaf from Lycurgus when he sat down to eat saying, "Treason does not keep company with a simple meal like this." After all, only a tasteless or stupid person would bring silver-footed couches, purple cushions, golden drinking bowls, and other such luxuries into a humble, rough-hewn home. No, the couch was bound to be compatible with the house, the fabrics compatible with the couch, and so on with all the rest of the decor and furnishings. **Leotychidas the Elder** gave expression to this custom when once dining in Corinth and noticing there the perfectly coffered ceilings. "What," he said, "do the trees grow square in your country!?"

A third rhetra forbade the Spartans from going to war too often against the same enemy lest their enemies get used to defending themselves and come to learn the arts of war from them. Later on this is precisely what they accused their king Agesilaus of doing. His frequent and prolonged campaigns against Boeotia made the Thebans a match for the Lacedaemonians. This is why, seeing his king wounded, Antalcidas said, "A fine lesson you have now received at the hands of the Thebans, whom you taught to fight—something they never wanted or knew how to do!"

These then are the rhetras, so named in the belief that they came from the gods as oracles.

NOTES

Lawgiver's intentions: Clearly a crucial sentence for Plutarch and one that employs many of the key terms, for example, resolution (*proairesis*) opposed to constraint (*ananke*), used by Aristotle in the *Nicomachean Ethics* and *Politics*. He goes on to attribute to Lycurgus the Aristotelian notion that all legislative systems tend to weaken as they become encumbered with minutia and constant amendment.

Competent: Plutarch's *pepaideumenoi*, or literally "those who have been educated," picks up the education (*agoge*) and upbringing (*paideusis*) of the previous sentence.

Leotychidas the Elder: Leotychidas I, a Eurypontid king, is thought to have reigned in the last quarter of the seventh century (Forrest 21).

[14] Convinced that **education** is the chief concern and noblest task of the lawgiver, Lycurgus started right at the beginning with regulations for marriage and childbirth. He did not, as Aristotle claims, give up on his attempts to tame the behavior of women who, due to their husbands' long absences from the home on military service, were of necessity left in charge and accustomed to having their own way and being addressed with overmuch respect (by the household slaves) as "Your Ladyship" or "Your Highness." Not at all. He gave this issue his full attention by prescribing a rigorous workout plan for young women that included running, wrestling, and javelin and discus throwing. In this way babies would be planted and grow in strong and healthy bodies and women would enjoy beautiful pregnancies and more easily undergo the labors of childbirth. He also removed those parts of a girl's education that encouraged softness, deference and girlishness, and insisted instead that girls be expected, like boys, to parade naked to the temple in the Gymnopaedia and to **sing and dance** in certain religious ceremonies with the young men all the while looking on. The girls might even taunt a boy by name with an apt comment when catching him in a mistake, or in their songs they might single out someone for praise and thereby inspire a great **love of honor** and a competitive spirit in the young men. Those who heard themselves praised for their manly achievements and celebrity among the girls walked away bursting with pride, while those who were the targets of even the most light-hearted teasing felt as though they had received a devastating reprimand, the more so because all the citizens, including the kings and elders, attended these processions to the goddess.

The Spartans never regarded a girl's nakedness as shameful. There was nothing lewd or vulgar about it. Only a natural modesty. Rather it instilled in girls a habit of simplicity and a desire for fitness while giving their sex a pride in excellence and a love of honor as deserving of them as of men. It is not surprising, then, that Spartan women would say the sort of thing attributed to Gorgo, the wife of Leonidas. When someone, probably a foreigner, said to her, "You Spartans are the only women who give orders to men," she replied, "We're the only women who give *birth* to men."

NOTES

Education: The Greek term *paideia*—and the Romance languages' use of the Latinate "education" for that matter, unlike English—does not necessarily or exclusively conjure up schooling and includes what we would call upbringing and child rearing. It can also be translated as "culture."

Sing and dance: Compare the Spartan poet Alcman's *Partheneia*, choruses for young girls. Here, for example, a fragment quoted by Antigonus in Edmonds' Loeb translation:

> *O maidens of honey voice so loud and clear, my limbs can carry me no more.*
> *Would O would God I were but a ceryl, such as flies fearless of heart with the halcyons over the bloom of the wave, the Spring's own bird that is purple as the sea!*

Love of honor: The celebrated Greek *philotimia* (love of honor). For the Greeks, a false modesty (*eironia* from which the English word "irony" derives), as seen in Theophrastus' character sketches, is a vice. This character is often translated into English as *The Hypocrite*. As the French say, "*ne vous faites pas si petit, vous n'êtes pas si grand*" (Don't make yourself so small, you're not that big).

[15] These public processions when the girls appeared without their clothes singing and dancing and competing in athletic contests encouraged the young men—enflamed by passion, as **Plato says**, rather than by reason—to marry. In fact, Lycurgus regarded celibacy as dishonorable and his laws discouraged it. Bachelors were not allowed to attend these public processions, and in wintertime the archons ordered them to walk around the marketplace naked while singing a song written to embarrass them and proclaiming that they deserved to be shamed in this way for having failed to marry. In addition, they were also stripped of the honor and respect that young men showed their elders. This is why, for example, no one was blamed for the rudeness shown to the well-respected general, Dercyllidas. As he entered the theater one day, a young man refused to offer him his seat saying, "What child of yours will some day offer me his seat?"

The Spartans marry by stealing a bride, not a child too young for marriage, but of ripe child-bearing years. Another woman they call the bridesmaid takes charge of the stolen bride, shaves her head, dresses her in a man's tunic and sandals, and leaves her lying alone on a straw mat in a dark room. The bridegroom, not intoxicated, but sober and composed, after having dined as usual with his cohort, enters her room, loosens her belt, and pledging his troth carries her to bed. After spending a short time with his bride, he leaves discretely and returns to the sleeping quarters of the young men. And he continues in this way, spending his days and nights in the company of his male companions and visiting his bride only in secret, taking every precaution not to be observed. His bride, meanwhile, helps him by looking for occasions and finding ways they can come together without being discovered. This pattern can continue for a long time. Some even have children before husbands see their wives in the light of day! These difficult and infrequent meetings not only provided training in moderation and restraint, but they assisted in fertility by making the couple's affection and desire for each other always fresh, and neither sated nor dulled by constant contact. When they parted, there was always something remaining, a smoldering flame of desire that kept their love for each other alive.

NOTES

Plato says: The allusion is to *Republic* 458D.

Having in this way assured mutual respect and restraint in marriage, Lycurgus with equal diligence sought to free it from the vain and womanish feelings of jealousy. To this end, he encouraged men to share their wives with others whom they thought deserving for the purpose of procreating children. He regarded as ridiculous those who demanded an exclusive right to their wives and out of jealousy would murder or **go to war** to defend that "right." It was possible, for example, for an older man with a young wife to invite a young man whom he admired to produce a child by her and be adopted as a child of his own. It was also possible for a man of good character who loved another man's wife for her modesty and fine children to persuade her husband to allow him to have a child by her and in this way, so to speak, sow his seed in fertile ground and produce children that shared the good bloodlines of both families.

Understand, in the first place, that Lycurgus considered children not as the property of their fathers, but as the common property of the state. For this reason, he wanted to make sure that the citizens of the state were bred from the best stock and not just anyone. He dismissed as utterly stupid and hypocritical the customs of others who take great pains and pay large sums to breed their horses and dogs with only the finest studs while shutting their wives up in their homes, to be the mothers only of their own children, even if they themselves are dimwitted, decrepit, and diseased. It is after all in the interest of everyone to have well-bred children since the challenge of raising sickly children of inferior breeding falls on their parents just as the pleasure of raising healthy children is the good fortune of their parents. These practices—believed to be perfectly natural and in the public interest —were at the time so far removed from what later became the reputation of Spartan women for promiscuity that they had no notion of adultery. There is a story told about Geradas, a Spartan from long ago, who was asked by a visitor the penalty for committing adultery. "Stranger," said Geradas, "nobody commits adultery here." "But what if someone should?" "Well," Geradas responded, "we would probably have to purchase a bull that could reach from the top of the Taygetus mountains to drink from

NOTES

Go to war: An ancient reader would immediately think of the Trojan War and perhaps the opening of Herodotus' *Histories*.

Marble relief fragment with scenes from the Trojan War
This piece is part of a series of tablets showing tiny relief scenes from the Trojan War. It is signed on the back by a Greek artist named Theodoros, who worked in Italy.
The Met Fifth Avenue in Gallery 171. (Public Domain Image)

the river Eurotas." The dumbfounded visitor exclaimed, "How could an animal possibly be that big?!" Geradas, laughing, answered, "How could someone commit adultery in Sparta?" So, this is what is recorded concerning Lycurgus' views on marriage.

[16] It was not assumed that the father automatically had authority to raise his child. Instead he was expected to take it to the club where the elders of his tribe met. They would examine the baby, and if they found it strong and well formed, they would give the father instructions on how he was to raise the child and assign one of the **nine thousand plots of land** for its support. But if the baby was frail or ill shaped, they would send it to the Dump, a deep ravine in the Taygetus mountains, thinking that it was not in the best interest of either the child or the state for it to live if not fit and strong from the very start. For this reason, Spartan women washed their newborns with wine rather than water as a kind of test of their strength. Apparently, they believed that a sickly baby or one prone to epilepsy would suffer convulsions if bathed in undiluted wine, while a wine bath will toughen and temper a healthy baby.

The Spartans paid special attention to the training of nurses. They taught them never to swaddle their babies, but to leave their limbs and bodies entirely free and unconstrained. They made sure their children were not picky about what they ate, not afraid of the dark or of being left alone, and not weepy or given to temper tantrums. It was training like this that made Spartan wet nurses sought after by some foreigners. Alcibiades the Athenian's wet nurse, Amycla, for example, was a Spartan. He was not so fortunate in his tutor, however. According to Plato, Pericles appointed just a common slave, Zopyros, for this task.

Lycurgus, on the other hand, refused to assign Spartan children to hired tutors or to put slaves in charge of them. Not even fathers were at liberty to raise their children as they pleased. Instead, when the children turned seven, Lycurgus took charge of them himself, teaching them how to get along with one another by dividing them into companies that ate, played,

Nine thousand plots of land: These nine thousand plots, worked by slaves that the Spartans called helots and owned by the Spartiates, were the foundation of the Spartan economy and political system. (See section [8] above.)

Ancient Roman Mosaic This mosaic shows the measuring of grains after harvest. *(Public Domain Image, Wikicommons)*

studied, and exercised together under the same rules and regimen. A boy, marked by his superior intelligence and physical toughness, is designated company leader. Everyone looks to him, obeys his orders, and submits to his punishments, so that the entire education becomes training in obedience. The older men keep a close eye on them and often provoke quarrels or contests among them in order to discover under stress the character of each boy, his degree of daring, and whether or not he will back down in a fight.

They learned only what reading and writing they needed to get by, and the rest of their education consisted of lessons in unquestioning obedience, indifference to hardship and pain, and the ability to win in battle. For this reason, as they grew older their training became more intense: Shaving their heads, marching barefoot, and usually playing naked. By the age of twelve, they already lived without underclothes and were given only a single cloak to last the entire year. Their skin was dried out and caked with dirt for they neither bathed nor used oil, except for a few days each year when they were vouchsafed this luxury. They slept together in small groups on mats of their own making from reeds growing on the banks of the Eurotas. They would break these off at the base without the use of a knife. In winter they inserted plants called *lycophons* under the mats and between these reeds to add warmth.

[17] Men formed **bonds of affection** with the boys they already admired at this young age. The older men also paid special attention to these lads, visiting their schools and attending their wrestling matches and their battles of wit, for they considered themselves to be the fathers, tutors, and guardians of all the boys. As a result, there was never an occasion or a place where there was not someone on hand to correct or punish a mistake.

Besides these arrangements, there was also a more formal provision for oversight and governance. A superintendent of education was selected from among the city's most prominent and respected men. He divided the boys into companies and placed over each company a captain, drawn from the

NOTES

Bonds of affection: Plutarch is referring to the relationship between a man called an *erastes* (lover) and an adolescent boy called an *eroumenos* (beloved) common to the aristocracy in virtually all Greek city-states but especially well-known and formalized among the warrior classes in Lycurgan Sparta and later in Thebes. To understand its importance we need to first recognize that a tutor (Greek "pedagogue") was by definition a slave and that teachers (Greek "sophists") who took all comers for a fee were scorned by the Greek aristocrat. In an aristocratic warrior society, a young man and future warrior could have no better teacher than an experienced warrior he looked up to as a hero, and an older warrior could have no better inspiration to act like one than to be treated as such by a gifted young admirer. The relationship was in theory exactly this and was considered perfectly normal in Greek society. That it sometimes involved sexual activity is certainly implied in the names (*erastes, eroumenos*) and it was known to occasionally inspire jealousy and violence, none of which is particularly surprising in the all-male and highly competitive closed societies involved. See the excellent discussion in H.I. Marrou's *A History of Education in Antiquity*, 50ff.

ranks of the *eirens* and chosen for his cunning and courage. (They call *eirens* the young men who are at least one year out of the boys' class, and *melleirens* those in their final year.) This *eiren*, at twenty years of age, commands his charges in combat and in the houses uses them to help prepare the meals. He orders the stronger boys to gather wood and the smaller ones to pick vegetables. This they do by raiding private gardens or by sneaking—with extreme cunning and caution of course—into the men's mess halls. Any boy caught stealing in this way can expect a severe beating, his penalty for being an inept or careless thief. In fact, they steal food whenever they can; this is how they learn to attack those who are asleep or off their guard. The boy who is caught not only receives a beating, but he goes hungry since most of his food comes from what he steals. This is how he learns not to expect handouts, but by his own cleverness and initiative to take care of himself. Another reason for their meager food allowance, they say, is to facilitate growth. Large quantities of food enervate and weigh down the vital spirit that makes men grow tall. Too much food and the body thickens and spreads out rather than rising upward as light things naturally do. A lean diet also produces beautiful bodies. Whereas it is easy to trace the fine features of a slender body, everything loses its shape and is covered up by obesity. This also explains why women who purge during pregnancy deliver more slender and attractive babies, **the matter** they provide being light and not weighing down the vital spirit shaping it. But I will leave this theorizing to others.

[18] Illustrating the deadly seriousness of this stealing business is the story of the boy who stole a fox cub and hid it under his cloak. Rather than be found out, he suffered the fox to rip out his guts with its claws and teeth, and dropped dead on the spot. We have no problem believing stories like this since we have seen many young men die from beatings at the altar of **Artemis Orthia.**

After dinner the *eiren* captain reclines on his couch and orders one of the boys to sing a song, and to another he puts a question that demands a careful

NOTES

The matter: The Greeks believed that the woman provided matter or raw material, which was shaped and given life by a man's seed.

Artemis Orthia: It was from the temple of Artemis Orthia, a fertility goddess, that the boys were supposed to practice by stealing sacred cheeses and where, apparently, the beatings took place if they got caught. For his own day, Plutarch uses the common Greek term *ephebes* to designate the eighteen-to-twenty-year-olds who underwent military training.

response. "Who is the best man in Sparta?" or "What is your opinion of so-and-so's behavior?" This started the boys out while still young judging the behavior of others, whether admirable or disreputable, and taking an active interest in what their fellow citizens were up to. A failure to have ready answers to questions like these was taken as a sign of laziness or attenuated ambition.

The right answer will be concise and to the point, well-reasoned, comprehensive, and persuasive. The boy whose answer is incorrect or poorly constructed will have his thumb bitten by the captain, who often invites older men and other captains to look on as he punishes his charges so that they can judge the fairness of his discipline, whether it is unreasonable or excessive. He is never stopped while administering a punishment, but once the boys have left he may expect to be reprimanded if his punishments were either unnecessarily harsh or too weak and gentle.

The **erastai** share the reputation, good or bad, of the boys they love. There is a story about a lad who cried out in pain during a fight, and for this the generals punished his *erastes*. Pederasty was so much a way of life in Sparta that the women also developed close bonds with young girls. Rivalry in these relationships did not exist. Rather, they tended to create friendships between *erastes* who loved the same boy and worked together to help him excel.

[19] They taught the boys to combine a sharp wit with graceful expression and to pack much thought into as few words as possible. In contrast to the little value he placed upon a lot of iron coinage, Lycurgus expected a simple, pithy speech to be full of valuable and useful ideas. His boys, accustomed as they were to long periods of silence, learned to give pointed and clever responses. Just as the sperm of philanderers is sterile, so the speech of those who are unable to control their tongues is void of sense. Once when an Athenian was making fun of the Spartan swords for being so short, suggesting that their proper use was in the theatre by the sword-swallowers, king Agis responded, "They're long enough to reach our enemies." Like the

NOTES

Erastai: See note "Bonds of affection" page 57.

Lead Figure of a Woman, late seventh to early fifth century BC
Over one hundred thousand small flat votive figurines of cast lead such as this one have been found in Laconia. They are thought to be dedicated to the godess Artemis Orthia in Sparta. Few images of women or children appeared on Greek and Roman pottery. Most images of women represent goddesses. (Laconia was the principal region of the Spartan state and was a part of the Roman Empire from the early second century BC until AD 395.)
The Met Fifth Avenue. (Public Domain Image)

Spartan sword, as I see it, Laconic speech is just long enough to cut to the quick and strike the minds of its listeners.

Lycurgus himself is remembered as a man of few but pointed words. Take, for example, his defense of the Spartan constitution to the man who wanted him to set up a democracy: "Why don't you try setting it up in your own family first?" And then there is what he said to the fellow who wanted to know why he allowed such small and inexpensive sacrifices to the gods: "So that we may never run out of things to offer them." Or what he said when asked what sorts of martial exercises and athletic competitions he approved of: "All of them, except those that end in the **raising of hands**." There are also the responses in letters he wrote to his fellow citizens. To the one asking, "How are we to defend ourselves against the attacks of our enemies?" he wrote, "Stay poor and don't desire more than the next fellow." And to someone else wanting to know why Sparta was not protected by a wall, he replied, "The best defense is a wall of men, not stones." As for these letters and the other sayings ascribed to Lycurgus, we cannot be sure whether they are real or counterfeit.

[20] Here are more examples of Spartan loathing of long speeches. When amidst a discussion on some important topic someone offered a clever but irrelevant remark, King Leonidas said, "Bull's eye, stranger, on the wrong target." When Charilaos, Lycurgus' nephew, was asked why his uncle made so few laws, he replied, "Men of few words need few laws." When the sophist Hecataeus was criticized for saying nothing during the common meal to which he had been invited, Archidamidas defended him by saying, "A man who knows what to say also knows when to say it."

Here are further examples of sharp wit combined with graceful expression: Damartos, hounded by some bothersome rascal who kept asking him to name the best Spartan, finally replied, "The one least like you!" Overhearing the Eleans being praised for their efficient and fair management of the Olympic Games, Agis remarked, "Yes, very impressive for the Eleans to be efficient and fair one day out of every four years." When a visitor to

Raising of hands: Raising or stretching out of hands was also a form of surrender in the ancient world.

Sparta, boasting of his affection for Lacedaemon, claimed that back home he was called "a friend of Sparta," Theopompus observed, "It would bring you more honor, stranger, to be called a friend of your own country." Upon hearing an Athenian orator go on about how the Lacedaemonians lacked learning, Pleistonax, the son of Pausanias, said, "How right you are! We are the only Greeks who have not learned your evil ways." And when asked how many Spartans there were, Archidamas responded, "Enough, stranger, to keep the wicked away."

Even in their jests the Spartans show this habit of saying something worth thinking about in just a few words. We are told that the Spartan response to being urged to listen to someone do a good imitation of a nightingale was, "We've heard nightingales sing." Another Spartan commented, upon reading this inscription on a tomb,

> *Here lie buried those whom bronze-clad Ares*
> *Slaughtered at the gates of* **Selinus**
> *While fighting to extinguish the flames of tyranny*

"They got what they deserved. Instead of quenching the fire, they should have let it burn the tyranny to the ground." A Spartan lad, once offered some gamecocks he was promised would "fight to the death," declined the offer saying, "I want cocks that will fight . . . and *live*." And another, seeing people sitting in a latrine relieving themselves, said, "May I never find myself seated in a place where I cannot give up my seat to someone older." All in all, apothegms like these support those who say, as some do, that **a love of wisdom** comes closer to describing the essential Laconic attribute than the love of exercise.

[21] No less intense than their zeal for the perfectly tuned speech was their instruction in poetry and song. Their songs breathed life into them, awakened their courage, and spurred them to take action. The

Selinus: Modern Selinunte, a once prosperous Greek city on the southern coast of Sicily. The Selinuntines were aided by the Spartan Euryleon in overthrowing the tyrant Peithagoras in the late-sixth century BC. The city was captured and the majority of its citizens massacred by the Carthaginians in 409 BC. A remnant was allowed to reoccupy the city, which was again destroyed by the Carthaginians during the First Punic War and never rebuilt. It remains, however, a spectacular ruin.

A love of wisdom: Plutarch cites Plato's judgment verbatim in the *Protagoras* 342e.

style of their songs was simple and plain and without embellishments; the subject matter serious and sententious. For the most part, their songs praised those who had died fighting for Sparta and covered themselves with glory and honor, or made a mockery of cowards who ever afterward lived in ignominy and shame. Depending on the age of the singers, their songs either boasted of the feats they would perform or of the conquests they had achieved. It may be helpful at this point to describe in detail one of these songs. In their festivals they form three choirs corresponding to three age groups. The chorus of older men begins like this:

We once were young, fearless, and strong.

The full-throated young men then respond:

Just as we are now. If you like, put us to the test.

And finally the children chime in, singing:

Someday we will be the strongest and bravest by far.

After a study of Laconian lyrics (some of which have survived to our day) accompanied by marching tunes played on a flute as the Spartans go into battle, one would have to agree with Terpander and Pindar that courage and poetry make good companions. Of Sparta, Terpander wrote:

The spear and song in her do meet,
And justice walks about her street;

And **Pindar**:

Councils of wise elders here,
And the young men's conquering spear,
And dance, and song, and joy appear.

NOTES

Style of their songs: Greek music was composed in different modes, still used in Western music today, depending on where a scale begins and how its steps are arranged. In Plato's *Republic* he argues that the different modes go to producing different forms of behavior, and at 399a (and see Adam, note 4), he has Socrates choose the Dorian mode for the warrior class in his ideal republic for its ability to abet warlike action and bravery.

Pindar: The translation of these verses from Terpander and Pindar is taken from Knightly Chetwood.

These poets show the Spartans to be as musical as they are warlike, a theme echoed by **one of their own poets**:

The sweet cithara walks alongside the iron spear.

Indeed, before going into battle, the king made sacrifice to the Muses, probably to remind his warriors of what their education had taught them—courage in the face of danger and the glory to be won by fighting bravely.

[22] On these occasions they relaxed the severe rules that governed the young men's training, and they allowed them to spruce up their hair, polish their weaponry, and sport fine clothes. They loved to see them in battle array prancing and pawing the ground like spirited horses. With the onset of formal military training at age eighteen, the young men began to wear their hair long, and when preparing for battle they took special care of their grooming, oiling their hair to make it glisten and dividing it into two thick long plaits, recalling what Lycurgus once said about long hair: that it made the handsome more beautiful and the ugly more terrifying. Their physical training along with the rest of their usually strict regimen was also relaxed while they were on campaign. All of this combined to make them the only men for whom war was a welcome respite from a hard life of training for war.

Once they were drawn up in **phalanx formation** and within sight of the enemy, the king would slaughter a young goat, command his warriors to don their laurel crowns, and order the flutes to pipe Castor's Air. He would then signal the advance by introducing the marching paean. It was at once a magnificent yet terrifying spectacle, to see these men in rank upon rank of unbroken lines marching calmly and joyfully into bloody battle to the lilting strains of their flutes. It stands to reason that men, their minds fortified in this way by sober hope and bright confidence in the favor of the gods, would engage the enemy without fear or frenzy.

NOTES

One of their own poets: This passage is from the Spartan poet Alcman. He is the earliest Greek choral poet whose work survives. His place of origin is disputed, but he produced his choruses in Sparta in the middle or second half of the seventh century, which, if our dating of Lycurgus is correct, makes them likely contemporaries.

Phalanx formation: Greek soldiers in the ancient world were called *hoplites*. Typically, they armed themselves with a long spear, a long shield, a short sword, a helmet that covered part of the face, a *cuirass* (breastplate) and *greaves* (shin guards). They fought shoulder to shoulder in a formation called the phalanx, each man's shield protecting his neighbor's right side. Depending on the shape of the battlefield and the number of hoplites, the object was to make the phalanx long enough so that it could not be outflanked and to build as many phalanx layers as possible in order to strengthen the force of the attack and provide replacement support for those in the front line whenever they tired or fell. The heavy bronze-clad shields, when placed side by side, formed a sort of wall over which the hoplites thrust their spears down upon the enemy. When fighting the Persians at Thermopylae, according to Herodotus, the spears of the taller Spartans punctured and carried off the leather caps of the Persians, becoming heavier and heavier as the battle wore on. Of course, when Greek hoplites opposed other Greeks, a more typical tactic was either through brute force to cause a breach in the opposing shield wall or to outmaneuver the enemy and seek to outflank him and thereby expose the side of his phalanx. Once the shield wall is breached or outflanked, the hoplite is no longer protected from the enemy's short sword, and his natural instinct is to throw down his heavy shield and run, a response discouraged by those standing in the phalanx behind him. This gives meaning to the Spartan mother's farewell to her son as he marched off to war: "Return with your shield or on it."

Hoplites: Illustration showing hoplites with weapons and gear for battle. Notice the left hoplite's shield has a curtain which serves as a protection from arrows. *(Public Domain Image, Wikicommons)*

The king himself advanced on the enemy in the close company of the men who wore **Olympic crowns**. The story is told of one of these men that he was offered a great sum of money if he would fail to show up at the Games. He refused, and after winning a very hard-fought contest, a spectator taunted him by asking, "So, Spartan, what have you to show for having fought and won?" His retort, beaming, "I shall now fight our enemies next to my king."

After outflanking or bursting through the enemy's phalanx and forcing him to retreat, they pursued him just long enough to be assured of the victory. Then they immediately withdrew, considering it ignoble and un-Greek-like to wound and slaughter those who have given up and stopped fighting. This way of dealing with their enemies was not only magnanimous, but smart. Those who fought against Spartans, knowing that it was their custom to carry off the corpses of those who resisted them and to spare the lives of those who surrendered, considered that the better part of valor was to flee.

[23] The sophist Hippias claims that Lycurgus was a great soldier and seasoned veteran. Philostephanus credits Lycurgus with organizing the Spartan cavalry into squadrons of fifty horse each and formed in squares. Demetrius of Phaleron, on the other hand, says that he never went to war and established his constitution during a time of peace. This makes more sense, especially if Lycurgus, as is commonly believed, procured the Olympic holy truce, or cessation of arms. But Hermippus complicates this picture by reporting that it was Iphitos, not Lycurgus, who proposed and procured the truce. He says that Lycurgus just happened to be attending the Games as a spectator when he heard a voice behind him blaming him for not encouraging his countrymen to leave off fighting and participate in the Games. Turning around, he saw no one and reckoned that it was

NOTES

Olympic crowns: Plutarch explains elsewhere (*Quaestiones Convivales* 639e) that the victory crown (and therefore the privilege to stand with the king) was reserved for contests with no monetary compensation.

Laurel Wreath: The laurel wreath is associated with the Greek god Apollo. It was given to victors in Olympic Games and to graduates in academia. It has been a symbol of praise and scholarship since the days of ancient Greece. Philosophers and those of the highest status were often depicted wearing a laurel wreath.

the voice of a god. He then sought out Iphitos and assisted him in reorganizing the **Festivities** and making them more secure, reputable, and dignified.

[24] A Spartan's education lasted well into his adulthood and never allowed him to live just as he pleased. He lived in what was, in effect, a military encampment: his way of life highly regimented and communal. He saw himself not as someone living as he pleases but as a subject of the state, serving the state's interests rather than his own. Unless he was assigned some other task, he spent his time attending to the children, teaching them something useful, or he would seek out the company of older men, hoping to learn something from them. This was one of the great blessings Lycurgus bestowed upon his fellow citizens: an abundance of **free time**. He accomplished this by forbidding them to engage in any form of craft or manual labor and, as we have seen, by making wealth unenviable and dishonorable and thereby freeing them from the irksome business of trying to make a living. That job was reserved for the helots who worked the land and produced enough to feed their families and pay the rents that supported the Spartan landowners. A story is told about a Spartan who found himself in Athens during the time when the courts were in session. He heard that someone had been found guilty and fined for failing to work and was being consoled by friends who sympathized with him and shared his grief. He asked his companion to point out the poor fellow who was being forced to pay a fine "for living like a free man." For a Spartan, freedom meant having free time; only a slave would spend his time working and making money. The Athenians might spend their time arguing in court, but the courts in Sparta disappeared along with the love of money since the equal sharing of the state's wealth and the modesty of everyone's needs caused the disparity between rich and poor to disappear. Instead, whenever they were not at war, the Spartans spent their wealth of free time in choral festivals and dances, hunting trips and feasts, sporting events and exercising, and in public discourse.

NOTES

Festivities: We have translated Plutarch's use the Greek word *panegyric* as Festivities. In ancient Greek this term meant a general assembly and came to be associated with the speeches given on such occasions. It is important to remember that the Olympic festival was first and foremost a religious one, in honor of Zeus. It involved sacrifices, speeches, diplomacy, and games, all in honor of the reigning god of Olympus. It is tempting to place this incident recorded by Plutarch at the opening ceremony, where Lycurgus might have been in attendance, but the Spartan athletes had not yet arrived. A similar situation seems to have occurred at the beginning of the Second Peloponnesian War, as recorded by Thucydides (V.49), when the Elians complained that the Spartans had broken the Olympic truce in their siege of Lepreum while the Spartans claimed that their siege ended before the truce started.

Free time: *Schole*, Latin *otium*, often translated as leisure or ease, could also designate the way leisure was used, in discussion or attending a lecture, and so becomes Aristotle's and our word "school." Its importance to Greco-Roman civilization cannot be overstated. What Plutarch goes on to describe as the freedom from manual labor and the need to work for a living was true of virtually all full citizens in the Greco-Roman world. They and their household of slaves lived off the excess produced by what was essentially a peasant economy, that which was produced in the countryside by the invisible majority of the Greco-Roman world, ranging from armies of slaves on great estates to freeholders like the Spartan *perioikoi*. This excess, slender as it sometimes was by modern standards, produced the urban civilization whose vestiges we admire and, thanks to *schole*, the literature and learning upon which the Western tradition is founded. On this question in general see De Sainte Croix IV *et passim*.

[25] Men under thirty years of age never went to the marketplace. Their relatives or lovers purchased whatever they needed. The older men also avoided the market, considering it demeaning to waste their time shopping. Instead they spent most of their time at the gym exercising or in their clubs, the so-called *lesches*, engaged in conversations deemed respectable, or, in other words, never mentioning money matters or market deals. Most of their talk dwelt on the men and deeds worthy of praise or those deserving of censure, but all of it done in a lighthearted and jocular manner intended to offer constructive criticism rather than to condemn. Not even Lycurgus himself was excessively serious. According to Sosibios, he placed a small **statue of Laughter** in their clubs and softened the edge of their harsh and austere lifestyle by encouraging humor at their common meals and in their club talk.

In all these ways, he ensured that the citizens of Lacedaemon were neither willing nor able to live without one another, but like bees they served only the interests of the hive, swarming together about their leader and losing all sense of self-awareness in their febrile thirst for recognition and their pride in being Spartans. This attitude is seen in some of their sayings. For example, when Pedaritos was not selected to be one of **the Three Hundred**, he came away beaming with pride, saying how happy he was that the state possessed three hundred men better than himself. When Polystratidas led a Spartan delegation on an embassy to the **King of Persia**, the King's generals asked him, "Are you men here on your own, or do you speak for the citizens of Sparta?" "If we succeed," replied Polystratidas, "we speak for our fellow citizens. If we fail, only for ourselves." When some of the citizens of Amphipolis journeyed to Sparta to see the mother of **Brasidas**, she asked them if her son had died in a noble manner, worthy of Sparta. They responded by praising her son to the skies and saying there was no one in Sparta to equal him. "Don't say that," she responded. "Brasidas was a brave man and true, but there are many in Sparta better than he."

NOTES

Statue of Laughter: It might be helpful to note that the Greeks liked to personify qualities and emotions in their myths. A fine instructive example would be their name for the mother of the Muses, Memory (*Mnemosyne*).

The Three Hundred: This was the honor guard that accompanied the king on campaigns.

King of Persia: Known in Greek simply as "the King."

Brasidas: Thucydides' *Histories* gives us a well-documented and reliable account of Brasidas' brilliant generalship in the first decade of the Peloponnesian War. In a campaign in Thessaly he wrested Amphipolis from Athenian control, and he later died saving it from an attack by a superior Athenian force by means of a brilliant sortie, which left seven Spartans and six hundred Athenians dead. Amphipolis gave him a hero's burial and placed his tomb near their acropolis, both things highly unusual in Greek practice.

[26] The senators, as already noted, were originally chosen by Lycurgus from among the men who supported his reforms, but later he ordered that whenever a senator died he should be replaced by a man over sixty with the most outstanding reputation. There was no contest greater than this or more worth fighting for. Far more sought after than for being the fastest runner or the strongest wrestler, this prize went to the best and wisest man and lasted for life and gave him what really amounted to absolute political power—the final say in the lives of his fellow citizens over life and death, honor and dishonor, and all other matters of highest importance.

This is how the contest was held: An assembly of the people was called from which a group of men was selected and shut up inside a room near the assembly grounds. From inside this room they could not see or be seen by those outside; they could only hear their shouts of acclamation. (As was always the custom, the length and loudness of the applause would decide the outcome of the contest.) The contestants were then introduced, not altogether but one by one in an order decided by lot, and led through the assembly in silence until the signal for applause. (Those shut up in the room recorded on tablets the size of the applause without knowing who was being acclaimed, only that it was the first one entering, the second, the third, and so on.)

The man receiving the loudest acclamation from the citizens is proclaimed the winner. Crowned with a garland and followed by a crowd of young men singing his praises, he makes the rounds of the sanctuaries to give thanks to the gods. A large company of women also follows him, praising his virtues in song and telling the story of his happy life. Along the way, as he encounters his family and friends, they offer him something to eat with the words, "Our city honors you with these refreshments." Finally, he arrives at his cohort's mess and partakes of the common meal as usual, except that he is now given a second helping that he accepts and sets aside. At the conclusion of the meal, his female relatives gather outside the door of his mess, and summoning the woman he most admires, he gives her the portion he has set aside, saying that he wants to share the honor he has received with her. She is then applauded by the other women and led in triumph home.

NOTES

Lycurgus Bas Relief in the US House of Representatives
This is one of twenty-three marble relief portraits over the gallery doors of the House Chamber in the US Capitol depicting historical figures noted for their work in establishing the principles that underlie American law. They were installed when the chamber was remodeled in 1949-1950. Created in bas relief of white Vermont marble by seven different sculptors, the plaques each measure twenty-eight inches in diameter. All the portraits are arranged so that they face Moses. *(Public Domain Work of the US Federal Governement, Wikicommons image)*

[27] Lycurgus also made excellent arrangements for burying the dead. First of all, to put an end to superstitions about the dead, he allowed the dead to be buried within the city limits and even around the sanctuaries of the gods. Consequently, young Spartans grew up surrounded by the **tombs of the dead**. Made familiar with death in this way, they learned not to be troubled by it, afraid to touch a corpse or walk on a grave. Next, he forbade them from burying anything with the corpse, only to wrap it in a purple cloak and cover it with olive leaves. Only the name of a man who had fallen in battle or a woman who died in childbirth could be inscribed on a tomb. He limited the time allowed for mourning to eleven days. On the twelfth day, one was expected to make a sacrifice to Demeter and stop mourning. No one was allowed to be idle or left to his own devices. In even the smallest details of daily life, Lycurgus prescribed models to follow that inculcated habits of good behavior and deterred bad habits. Growing up in this environment, influenced by these models and formed by these habits, how could one fail to be programmed for virtue?

This also explains why he did not want Spartans to leave Lacedaemon and travel about freely, returning with bad habits acquired abroad and with manners picked up from those lacking a Spartan education or with different social and political norms. By the same token, he sought to prevent foreigners from slipping into the state, not—as **Thucydides claims**—because he feared they would learn something about excellence and attempt to copy the Spartan system, but because they would introduce bad habits and corrupt the citizens. With foreigners come **foreign words** and ideas—words and ideas that would inevitably excite passions and introduce **principles** in conflict with Spartan norms and ideals. For this reason Lycurgus regarded foreigners and their corrupting influences as **worse than the plague**.

[28] Now, **up to this point** there is no trace of injustice or inequality in Lycurgus' laws, but there are those who criticize his laws, saying that although they produce good soldiers, they are lacking in justice. They base

Tombs of the dead: A Greco-Roman cemetery, or necropolis, was placed outside the city walls, and memorial tombs typically lined the road outside the city gate, the prime example much visited today being the Via Appia Antica and the Catacombs leading out of Rome.

Thucydides claims: The reference is to a well-known passage (ii.39) in "Pericles' Funeral Oration" in which Pericles refers specifically to the Spartan policy of banishing strangers (*xenelasia*), in the Jowett translation: "Our city is thrown open to the world, and we never expel a foreigner or prevent him from seeing or learning anything of which the secret if revealed to an enemy might profit him." This is an instructive example of how Plutarch distorts his evidence to defend Sparta's reputation at the expense of Athens.

Foreign words: The word we translate as "words"—*logoi*, plural of logos—means reasoned speech or sometimes stories or accounts. It gives us the word "logic" and is given whole new significance by the opening of John's gospel: "In the beginning was the Logos and the Logos was with God and the Logos was God."

Principles: *Proairesis* again. See note on "Lawgiver's intentions," page 47.

Worse than the plague: Plato's inspiration is evident both in Plutarch's use of metaphors (music and medicine) and in the general argument (see *Laws* 950).

Up to this point: Plutarch simply uses the demonstrative pronoun, "these things," but he apparently is referring to what follows, perhaps in part referring as well to the last item mentioned, the *xenelasia*, which had also come under highly respected Greek criticism. Whatever the case, his introduction to this subject does not seem to fit his conclusion below.

their criticism on the so-called "secret police" (*krypteia*) of the Spartans, if—as Aristotle claims copying Plato—this really was one of Lycurgus' creations. Here is how it worked: The Spartan commanders would routinely send a group of the cleverest young men into the countryside armed only with a dagger and the barest necessities. By day they would hide out and rest, dispersed in various locations with good cover, and when night fell they would go down to the roads and slit the throats of any helots they caught. They would also attack the strongest helots and murder them while they were working in the fields. **In his history of the Peloponnesian Wars**, Thucydides tells how the Spartans used to single out and crown with garlands the bravest of the helots, promising them freedom and parading them through the temples. But shortly afterwards, they all mysteriously disappeared, over two thousand of them. How they perished no one could say, either then or now. Aristotle makes the point that the **ephors**, upon being sworn into office, declare war on the helots and thereby make it possible to murder them without angering the gods.

The Spartans treated the helots harshly and cruelly in other ways as well. Forcing them to drink huge quantities of undiluted wine, they would parade them through the mess halls as a way of showing the young men a revolting spectacle of drunkenness. They made them sing vulgar songs and dance obscene dances in order to mock them, and they forbade them from performing the songs and dances of free men. Later, when the **Thebans invaded Laconia** and asked the helots they had captured to entertain them by singing the songs of Terpander, Alcman, and Spendon, the helots refused to do so, saying, "Our Masters will not allow it." Hard to argue with the man who said, "There is no one more free than the free man in Sparta or more utterly enslaved than the slave there."

My own personal belief is that this cruel treatment of the helots came later than Lycurgus, especially after the great earthquake when the helots joined the Messenians in laying waste to the countryside and posing a serious threat to the city. I cannot bring myself to ascribe to Lycurgus such a **bloody** and barbaric institution as the *krypteia*, seeing elsewhere in his

NOTES

In his history of the Peloponnesian Wars: Other than the fact that Thucydides says the helots did the choosing, Plutarch follows Thucydides' account closely.

Ephors: The ephors were elected annually by the assembly. They accompanied, supporting and overseeing, the kings, presided at meetings of the senate, and had oversight over the *agege* and state in general. See section [7].

Thebans invaded Laconia: This would be after the Battle of Leuctra in 371 BC.

Bloody: The Greek word adds the ancient notion of ritual pollution for manslaughter.

character and laws a consistent habit of gentleness and justice to which the **gods** themselves bore witness.

[29] In time Lycurgus saw his most important reforms firmly established in Sparta and in the hearts and minds of its citizens, and he became confident that the security and well-being of the state no longer depended on him. Feeling the delight Plato ascribed to the Creator as the cosmos came into being and satisfied with the perfection and workings of his laws and ordinances, Lycurgus determined—to the extent humanly possible—to leave it all to posterity, fixed and timeless. So, gathering all the citizens together, he told them that now almost everything was in place for the **happiness and excellence** of the state, and that to provide the one thing of greatest importance still lacking he would have to consult the oracle. He made them promise to obey the laws as established without altering or revising them in any way until his return from Delphi. He promised to do whatever the god thought best as soon as he returned. They all readily agreed and urged him to be on his way. But before leaving, he made everyone—the kings and senators and all the people—swear by the gods that they would abide by and keep faith with his laws until he got back.

When he arrived at Delphi, he sacrificed to the god Apollo and asked the god if his laws were enough to guarantee the happiness and excellence of the state. The god replied that Lycurgus' laws were most excellent and that as long as the Spartans lived by them they would cover themselves and their state with glory. Lycurgus wrote down the oracle and had it sent to Sparta, having already decided never to release his fellow citizens from their oath and to end his life of his own free will where he was. He then sacrificed again to Apollo and embraced his friends and his son. Having reached **the age when life is on the cusp**, when to make an end or to carry on is no longer a matter of honor, he stopped eating and ended his life. He believed that even a statesman's death should benefit the state and that dying itself might be remembered as a final accomplishment and display of virtue. For himself, having completed the noble work he had set out to accomplish, his

NOTES

Gods: We are reminded that Plutarch was a priest of Apollo Pythian. See section [5].

Happiness and excellence: Plutarch's insistence on this combination, happiness and excellence, in Greek *eudaimonia* and *arete*, repeated below in Lycurgus' question to the oracle, is reminiscent of Aristotle's definition in the *Nicomachean Ethics* I.13 of happiness (*eudaimonia*) as the highest good after which men seek as "a certain activity of the soul in conformity with perfect virtue *(arete)*," which, it should be noted, is the ultimate source of Thomas Jefferson's "pursuit of happiness" in the Declaration of Independence. It also suggests the claim that Lycurgan Sparta managed to combine both the *heroic* highest good and the civic highest good as they were expressed in the ancient Greek tradition. The Homeric hero sought personal excellence *(arete)* in war, and Homer celebrated in song the hero's *aristeîa* or moment of valor. Our first account of happiness (*eudaimonia*) as a civic virtue is in Herodotus' *Histories* I.30ff., where the prosperous king of Lydia, Croesus, asks the Athenian lawgiver Solon to name the most blest man he knows, using the word *olbios*, which in Homer always refers to material wealth (see L&S *sub loc.*), thinking it must surely be himself. Solon responds by naming a normal Athenian citizen who had the good fortune to lead a full life and see his fine children grow up and give him grandchildren, ultimately dying in battle in the hoplite line with his fellow citizens in defense of the city. By the end of Herodotus' story, Solon has changed his key term to *eudaimonia*, redefining as civic virtue a word that also in Homeric usage implied material wealth.

The age when life is on the cusp: Other sources (the *Macrobii*, attributed to Lucian) tell us that Lycurgus lived to the age of eighty-five.

death rounded out a life of perfect bliss; and for his fellow citizens who had sworn to abide by his laws until his return, his death would secure for them and future generations the protection and benefits of his equable and just constitution. Nor was he off the mark in his calculations. For five hundred years and as long as the laws of Lycurgus were strictly observed, Sparta was far and away the top city in Greece in terms of stable government and sterling reputation. Fourteen kings came and went without a change until **the time of Agis**, the son of Archidamus. Even the ephorite innovation, initially thought to weaken the state by introducing a democratic element, actually increased the power of the aristocracy.

[30] **Money flowed into Sparta** for the first time in the reign of Agis, and with money came greed and the desire for wealth. Lysander, although personally incorruptible, caused this to happen when, ignoring the laws of Lycurgus, he returned to Sparta with the rich spoils of war, gold and silver, and filled his homeland with the love of money and luxury. So long as Sparta had the upper hand, it seemed to have not so much the laws of a state as the lifestyle of a disciplined and well-trained athlete. Or a better analogy might be the way the poets describe Herakles with his lion skin and his club, going about the land punishing lawless and bestial tyrants. Just so, Sparta, with a **simple staff** and a threadbare cloak, ruled a willing and grateful Greece by bringing down unjust power grabs and tyrannies, mediating her conflicts, and putting an end to her revolutions. It accomplished all this without dusting off a single shield, but merely by sending a lone ambassador whose orders everyone—like bees when the **queen** appears—hastened to obey. So far did Sparta excel all other states in its governance and justice.

I confess being perplexed by those who say that Spartans knew how to be ruled but never learned how to rule and who borrow a saying of King Theopompus to support their claim. When the king heard someone, probably trying to flatter him, say that Sparta owed its security and strength to kings who knew how to rule, he replied, "Rather to citizens willing to

NOTES

The time of Agis: Agis reigned from 427 to 400 BC.

Money flowed into Sparta: Plutarch's account of Sparta's decline after her defeat of Athens in the Peloponnesian Wars might be compared with Aristotle's judgment in his *Politics* 1271b.3-6: "The Spartans always prevailed in war but were destroyed by empire simply because they did not know how to use the leisure they had won, because they had practiced no more fundamental skill than skill in war."

Simple staff: The *skytale*, a special Spartan staff or cudgel wrapped slantwise with a leather roll on which military dispatches were written lengthwise in such a way as to be unintelligible when unrolled but could be wound and read on a receiving commander's staff (L&S *sub loc.*).

Queen: Like Aristotle, Plutarch in fact uses the masculine, mistaking the queen bee for a king bee. Others, like Xenophon, get it right.

obey and be ruled." No one wants to listen to those incapable of giving orders. A good leader instills in his followers the desire to obey. Just as the essential element in equestrian art is to render a horse gentle and obedient, the art of leadership comes down to making men willing to obey. But more than rendering other Greeks willing to obey, the Spartans made them eager to be ruled and follow their orders. They petitioned Sparta, not for ships or money or soldiers, but for a single commander whom they welcomed and treated with honor and respect. Such was the case with the Sicilians and Gylippus, with the Chalcidians and Brasidas, and with all the Greeks in Asia and Lysander, Callicratidas and Agesilaus. They called these men **composers** and imposers of sound rule and discipline on everyone, people and princes alike; and like young pupils they looked upon Sparta itself as a tutor and teacher of life well tuned and government well conducted. This must be the point of Stratonicus' parody of the lawgiver when he proposes that Athens celebrate the mysteries and be in charge of the sacred processions, that the Eleans run the Games, and the Spartans take the beating when others misbehave. That was just a joke, of course, but Antitheses the Socratic was not joking when he told the Thebans whom he heard boasting after the Battle of Leuctra, "You are no better than little schoolboys bragging about having beaten up your **teacher**."

[31] But creating a state that would govern others was not what Lycurgus had in mind. He believed that just as individuals are happy who practice virtue and possess inner peace, the happiness of the state demands virtuous citizens living together in harmony. Accordingly, he designed laws and instituted customs that would last and would form free, self-reliant, and self-regulated citizens. Plato, Diogenes, Zeno, and all the rest who wrote and taught on this subject agreed with his aims, but they left behind just books and lectures. Only Lycurgus created and left behind not books and lectures, but an actual and unique type of government. Lycurgus has shown those who doubt that man is capable of attaining to wisdom an entire state in love with wisdom. Is it any wonder that his reputation surpasses by far all those Greeks who ever presumed to spin political theories?

NOTES

Composers: *Harmosts*, from *harmaze*, which Plutarch follows Plato in using to mean to tune and create harmony.

Teacher: For the sake of poignancy, it helps to know that the job of a tutor (Greek "pedagogue") was to keep the boys from getting beaten up on their way to and from school.

For this reason Aristotle says that they honor him less than he deserves in Lacedaemon, even though they have built a temple in his honor and offer yearly sacrifices to him as to a god. It is reported that when his remains were carried back home to Sparta, lightning there struck his tomb. We do not know of this happening to anyone else of note other than Euripides, who died and was buried at Arethusa in Macedonia. The poet's admirers regard this as proof of the gods' special favor toward him since this happened only once before to Lycurgus, the lawgiver revered as most holy and beloved of the gods.

Some say Lycurgus died in Cirrha, but Apollothemis says he was taken to Elis and died there. Timaeus and Aristoxenus report that he ended his days in Crete. To support this claim, Aristoxenus adds that Cretans are in the habit of showing visitors his tomb along the Strangers Road in Pergamia. We are told that he left only one child, his son Antiorus, who died childless and ended his line. But for many years afterward his family and friends gathered annually to commemorate his death, calling the days when they met *Lycurgides*. Finally, Aristocrates, the son of Hipparchus, affirms that he died in Crete, but that according to his wishes, his Cretan hosts burned his body and scattered his ashes in the sea to prevent his remains from being returned to Lacedaemon and giving the Spartans a pretext for claiming that he had returned and they could be released from their pledge and begin tinkering with his laws.

That is what we know concerning Lycurgus.

Numa & the Nymph Illustration of the early Roman king Numa consulting with a nymph on various matters of state and religion. F.J. Gould, *"The Children's Plutarch: Tales of the Romans,"* 1910, frontispiece. (*Wikimedia Commons*)

The Life of
NUMA POMPILIUS

NUMA POMPILIUS

[1] Even though we have precise genealogies dating all the way back to King Numa's reign, there is, as with Lycurgus, wide disagreement about the time **when he lived**. A writer named Claudius in a book he titled *Refutation of Chronologies* asserts that Rome's ancient records disappeared when the Gauls sacked the city and that what we now have is counterfeit—made up by men who wished to curry favor with those wanting to trace their roots back to the city's first families and **most prestigious houses to which they did not belong**. As for the oft-told story that Numa was a disciple of Pythagoras, others state categorically that Numa had no knowledge whatsoever of Greek language or learning and that he was either naturally capable of attaining moral excellence on his own or that we should attribute his education to a **non-Greek** greater than Pythagoras. Yet others say that Pythagoras was born much later, about **five generations after Numa**, and that this confusion arises from the fact that there was another named Pythagoras, a Spartan who in the third year of Numa's reign won the ***stadion*** at the sixteenth Olymdiad. He met Numa while traveling in Italy and worked with him to perfect his constitution. This would explain why so many **Spartan laws and customs** are mixed in with the Roman ones. Besides, Numa was a Sabine by birth, and the Sabines claim descent from Lacedaemonian colonists. It is in any case difficult to base a chronology on the lists of Olympic winners since these lists were compiled much later by Hippias of Elis and lack a reliable starting point. We have made the best guess of where to begin and from there will report on what we have learned concerning the life of Numa.

[2] Rome had been settled under the kingship of Romulus for thirty-seven years when, on the fifth day of the fifth month, on the day now called Capratine Nones, Romulus was holding a public sacrifice outside the city at the Goat's Marsh in the presence of the Senate and the people of Rome. Suddenly, the heavens turned dark, and a thick cloud of rushing wind and rain descended on the earth. Fleeing in fright, the people scattered, and amidst all the commotion Romulus disappeared, never to be seen again

NOTES

When he lived: The Greeks possessed nothing comparable to the king-lists of Egypt and Mesopotamia dating as far back as 3150 B.C. They based their chronologies on the names of the Olympic victors dating back to the founding of the Games in 776 BC.

Most prestigious houses to which they did not belong: The student of Virgil's *Aeneid* will recall the poet's insistence on having the *gens Iulia*, the house of Augustus Caesar, descend from Aeneas' son Ascanius or Iulus and the especially memorable phrase in book 9.641 when Apollo addresses Ascanius as Iulus, *dis genite et geniture deos*, sired of gods and siring gods to come.

Non-Greek: Plutarch's word is *barbaros*, or barbarian, the Greek term for anyone who did not speak Greek and whose speech to a Greek sounded like bar-bar-bar-bar.

Five generations after Numa: Pythagoras lived 150 years after the time ascribed to Numa, a fact worth bearing in mind when reading the claims reported in section [8].

Stadion: The *stadion* was the original and remained the most prestigious race of the ancient Olympic Games, a sprint in the stadium of 210 yards.

Spartan laws and customs: Other than the general focus on military prowess, the sovereignty of Senate and *Gerousia*, twin consulships and twin kingships, and similar roles of plebeian tribunes and *ephors* struck the ancients as fairly unique and remarkably similar features.

either living or dead. A hostile suspicion soon attached to the patricians, and a nasty rumor began to circulate among the people that, disgruntled with the king's harsh treatment of them and wanting his power and authority for themselves, the patricians had done away with him. To put an end to these rumors, the patricians accorded divine honors to Romulus and said that **he had not died but been raised to a higher state**. In support of this claim, Proclus, a man of high standing in the community, swore that he had seen the king taken up into heaven in full armor, crying out as he ascended that he should hereafter be called by the name **Quirinus.**

Unrest and civil strife once again seized the city over the choice of the next king. The **Sabines**, newly joined to the city, did not yet form a perfect union with the original Romans, and the patricians out of jealousy and mutual suspicions also fought amongst themselves. Everyone agreed on the need for a king, but over who that man should be and from what tribe, they fought bitterly. Those who had founded and built the city with Romulus and had surrendered some of their lands to the Sabines when they took them in were outraged that these recipients of their generosity should now want to rule over them. At the same time, the Sabines' case was not without merit. When their king Tatius died, they did not rebel against Romulus and demand a king of their own, but allowed him to reign alone. Now, they reckoned, it was only fair for the next king to come from their tribe. After all, they had not joined Rome as inferiors either in strength or in numbers, and it was their decision to unite their peoples that put Rome on the map.

These then were the arguments that divided the city. To prevent these disputes from descending into anarchy and making the city ungovernable, the **patricians**, who were 150 in number, decided to rotate the office of supreme magistrate amongst themselves, ordering that each senator in turn wear the royal insignia, offer the customary sacrifices to the gods, and conduct the business of the city for six daylight and six nighttime hours. This arrangement appeased the patricians as it seemed

He had not died but been raised to a higher state: Worship of living rulers as gods was actually a practice the Romans picked up from the Greeks, for whom it had become standard practice from Alexander the Great on. We saw hints of it in the hero-founder cult given to Brasidas by the citizens of Amphipolis, and Plutarch says that the treatment of Lysander by the Ionians was the first example of it. Roman rulers in Greece accepted divine honors already in the second century BC, and Julius Caesar, who claimed descent from Venus, put the Senate in a tizzy by allowing himself to be called *divus Iulius* in Rome, although that was a title that by Roman practice had to be granted by a vote of the Senate and only after one's death. (Compare the nice irony of Vespasian on his death bed: *sentio ut deus fiam*—I sense I'm becoming a god.) Once the Senate voted that honor to Julius Caesar in 42 BC, Octavian had his temple built at the entrance to the forum and dedicated it in 27 BC after he had accepted the honorific title Augustus, or "Reverend," again on a vote by the Senate after the Battle of Actium in 31 BC. As had been done by Roman commanders in the Hellenistic east, living Roman emperors accepted divine honors in the eastern empire and occasionally in the western provinces—examples exist in Africa and Britain—but never in Rome. There tends to be confusion with the imperial cult, which Jews and Christians viewed as worshiping the living emperor as a god, as had been the case with Hellenistic monarchs.

Quirinus: The origin and meaning of this title has given rise to all sorts of conjectures, ancient and modern. We have the Quirinal Hill in Rome, which associates the name with the Sabines, and the word's origin may be related to the Sabine village of Cures, or to *curis*, the Sabine word for a spear; and all that may be connected to *Quirites*, an alternative term for Roman citizens. Quirinus was evidently an ancient Roman god, and an important one at that.

Sabines: Plutarch recounts the union of Romans and Sabines following the episode known as the Rape of the Sabines in his life of Romulus. Also in that life, Plutarch claims that the original Sabines were colonists from Sparta. This claim, whatever its merits, may be the basis for the connection Plutarch makes between Lycurgus' reforms and Numa's policies.

Patricians: Plutarch appears to be using the term *patrikioi* here to designate senators, but the terms patrician and senator are otherwise distinct. At this early period, the two were virtually synonymous since, according to Livy, the name "patrician" designates the families (and descendants, including adopted members—e.g., Octavian/Caesar Augustus—in perpetuity) of the original senators (*patres* in Latin). Livy says there were one hundred originally; Plutarch's 150 is another anomaly of his.

even-handed, and the way power changed hands pleased the people and removed any thoughts of envy. After all, in the space of a single day and night a man both ruled as king and joined the people as a private citizen. The Romans call this power-sharing arrangement an **interregnum**.

[3] Even though the senators appeared to govern moderately and in the interest of the city, the people began to grumble and suspect them of putting off the naming of a king in order to establish an oligarchy and manage the state for themselves. As a consequence, the two tribes came to an agreement. Each would choose a royal candidate from the other, the Sabines nominating a Roman and the Romans a Sabine. This, they believed, would end their rivalry and give them a king who would treat both sides fairly since he would love those who nominated him and be well disposed toward those from his own tribe. The Sabines deferred to the Romans, who preferred to choose a Sabine rather than allow the Sabines to select a Roman. In the event, after conferring with one another, the Romans nominated Numa Pompilius, a Sabine who had not come to live in Rome but one so famous for his virtue that the Sabines immediately accepted him as the best man to rule over them. Having announced this decision to the people, the senate sent the leading men from both tribes as ambassadors to invite him to come and be their king.

Now Numa lived in **Cures**, the principal city of the Sabines, from which the name Quirites for both Romans and Sabines derives. His father was the hugely respected Pompon, and he was the youngest of four brothers, born, as ordained by divine providence, on the same day as the founding of Rome under Romulus, **the eleventh day before the Kalends of May**. He was endowed by nature with a temperate character disposed to virtue. His disciplined and austere life and his study of philosophy only augmented his natural tendencies and banished from his soul not only the passions condemned by the Greeks, but also those like violence and greed viewed favorably by the barbarians. To what extent are the passions ruled by reason? That, he believed, is the real test of courage.

NOTES

Interregnum: The source for Plutarch's account of the interregnum is unknown. Cicero's account (*De Republica* 2.23) and Livy's account (*Ab urbe condita* I.17) have each senator reigning for five consecutive days.

Cures: See note "Quirinus" above. The resemblance works better in Plutarch's Greek, where the town is named after its citizens, the *Kyrites*, the Greek transliteration of the Latin *Quirites*.

The eleventh day before the Kalends of May: April 21, 753 BC in our dating. The Romans dated "from the founding of the city," *ab urbe condita*, or A.U.C.

Numa lived simply and without luxurious furnishings or an extravagant lifestyle at home. In his public life, he gained a reputation among citizens and foreigners alike as an incorruptible judge and wise counselor. In his private life, he used his **free time** not to pursue pleasure or make money, but to serve the gods and contemplate the reasons for their nature and power. So renowned for these traits was he that Tatius, the joint king with Romulus, chose him to marry his only daughter, Tatia. Nor did Numa take advantage of this fine marriage by moving to Rome and living with his father-in-law, but chose instead to stay with the Sabines and look after his aging father. Tatia also chose the quiet life of her husband, the private citizen, over the glorious and splendiferous life she might have enjoyed in her father's Rome. She is said to have died in the thirteenth year of her **marriage to Numa**.

[4] After this, Numa abandoned city life and moved to the country where he took long solitary walks through the forests and meadows and remote places consecrated to the gods. It was this habit that probably gave rise to the story about the goddess according to which **Numa abandoned human society not out of grief or some mental disorder but because he had found a more hallowed society**. Having been found worthy to marry a goddess, he wed the nymph Egeria, and having lived and made love with her, he attained blessedness and became wise in the ways of the gods. This story is not unlike the old legends that the Phygians tell about Attis, the Bithynians about Rhodoetes, the Carians about Endymion, and countless others thought blessed and beloved of the gods. And these tales make a certain sense. After all, why would the god, being a lover of men rather than of horses or birds, shun or disregard the company of men, especially one who is exceptionally good and wise? Yet it is hard to believe that a god or spirit could form a physical bond with a human body. The Egyptians, on the other hand, make a distinction between the ability of a god's breath to impregnate a woman and the inability of a man to have intercourse with a goddess. In this way they fail to understand the principle of reciprocity: when two things mix they exchange equally.

NOTES

Free time: *Schole*, free time or leisure, the essential condition of a free citizen according to the ancient Greeks. See note on "Free time" above, page 73.

Marriage to Numa: Plutarch comes back to Numa's marriage in section [21].

Numa abandoned human society . . . because he had found a more hallowed society: In Plutarch's account of the famous Roman legend of Numa and Egeria, we have a good example of what might be called a rationalizing Greek treatment, e.g., the Greek tendency to regard myths as primitive ways to describe natural phenomena or historical events. Compare Livy's account (*Ab urbe condita* I.21), which is less embellished and, even if he also says that Numa played it up, takes the story at face value, much as he does the yearly reports of prodigies. Plutarch's account (*Sertorius* 11) of the Roman general Sertorius' conversations with the goddess Diana in the form of a white fawn during his campaign against Pompey in Spain is similarly rationalizing. Again in the case of Sertorius, there is no reason to think that the Romans would not have accepted the story at face value.

Nonetheless, it is only reasonable for gods to have affection for men and for their love to be spoken of as sexual **desire**. Their love inspired these men to behave bravely and virtuously. Consider the stories of a Phorbas, a Hyacinth, an Admetus—all loved of Apollo—or Hippolytus of Sicyon. They say that every time he sailed to Cirrha from Sicyon, the Pythian priestess would chant **this heroic verse** expressive of the god's affection and joy:

The beloved head of Hippolytus again chances life upon the sea.

They also say that Pan fell in love with Pindar for his songs, and that for the sake of the Muses, the gods honored Archilochus and Hesiod after they died. There is another story about Sophocles, well testified to this day, that during his lifetime he received **Asclepius** as a guest in his home, and after he died another god arranged for his funeral. So, if we credit these stories about poets, why should we doubt that the gods also appeared to Zaleucus, Minos, **Zoroaster**, Numa, and Lycurgus, who ruled kingdoms and established orderly governments? Is it not reasonable to believe that the gods would offer wise instruction and advice to men seeking to do good, if indeed they also amused themselves with the warbling of lyrical songbirds? And if someone wants to argue the point, I say with Bacchylides, "broad is the path." Nor would I dismiss the argument of those who claim that Lycurgus, Numa, and other famous lawgivers who tried to reform their societies made up these stories about divine interventions in order to subdue a populace hard to please and difficult to control. Even if not true, their lies benefitted those who believed them.

[5] Numa was about forty years old when the ambassadors came from Rome inviting him to become king. Proclus and Velesius spoke for them. Proclus favored by the Romans, Velesius by the Sabines were the candidates otherwise most likely to be elected as king by the people. They spoke briefly, assuming that Numa would be delighted with his good fortune. But

NOTES

Desire: For a Christian example, we might point to the writings of Teresa of Ávila, *La Vida (The Way of Perfection)* and their inspiration for Bernini's famous *Ecstasy of Saint Teresa* sculpture in Santa Maria della Vittoria in Rome.

This heroic verse: A hexameter, the measure of epic poetry.

Asclepius: The cult of Asclepius, son of Apollo and god of healing, seems to have become popular in the late fifth and fourth centuries BC, when his sanctuary at Epidaurus, for example, became a major pilgrimage site. Sophocles introduced his cult in Athens and set up his altar in his home for which the Athenians gave him the posthumous title of *Dexion*, or Receiver.

Zoroaster: Zaleucus of Locri in southern Italy is credited with the earliest Greek law code, while Minos is the legendary king of the Minoans in Crete, and Zoroaster (or Zarathustra) the ancient Persian prophet and founder of Zoroastrianism, one of the world's earliest monotheistic religions.

in this assumption they were sorely mistaken and had to exhaust themselves in arguments and entreaties to persuade a man who led a calm and peaceful life to govern a city that had come into being and grown through war. In the presence of his father and of Marcius, one of his relatives, he responded thus:

> *Every change in a man's life is dangerous, and for someone who has everything he needs and is content with everything he has, it is nothing short of madness to rearrange his world and change his habits. Even if his habits offer no other advantage to him, they are still safer than venturing into the unknown. And the dangers of trying to govern Rome are certainly not unknown, considering how Romulus' reputation suffered when he was accused of plotting against his fellow king Tatius and the damage done to the reputation of the Senate when it later was accused of murdering Romulus. All of this in spite of Romulus' obvious advantages: praised in song as a child of the gods, divinely born and miraculously suckled by wolves. I, on the other hand, possess none of these advantages: I was born to mortals and suckled and raised by folks you know. The qualities for which I'm praised are far from those that befit a king: a love of tranquility and the study of impractical subjects, a fervent devotion to peace, an interest in matters unrelated to war, and a preference for the company of men who gather only to honor the gods and engage in quiet conversation and who otherwise spend their time tilling their fields and tending their cattle. Like it or not, you Romans have inherited many wars from Romulus, and your city will need a fiery king in his prime to fight its battles. Moreover, due to their good fortune, the ambition of your people and their desire to grow their kingdom and rule others are no secret. In short, I would be a laughing stock urging our citizens to worship the gods, love justice, and eschew violence and war in a city that needs a general more than it needs a king!*

NOTES

Plate 28: Mars on horseback and Romulus and Remus with the wolf at lower left
This engraving from Guillielmus Becanus' *Serenissimi Principis Ferdinandi, Hispaniarum Infantis* was created by Jacob Neeffs in 1636. *The Elisha Whittelsey Collection, The Elisha Whittelsey Fund, 1951, The Met. (Public Domain Image)*

[6] Sensing that with these words Numa was about to turn down the kingship, the Romans became more impassioned, insisting that he alone was the person on whom both Romans and Sabines could agree and that without him their city would be thrown back into disorder and internecine war. After the ambassadors had spoken and departed, Numa's father and Marcius also urged him to accept the kingship as a gift from heaven rather than from men, saying:

> *Although* **being content with what you have** *you do not wish for more and enjoying a reputation for virtue you have no need for the fame attached to leadership and power, you should at least consider the kingship as a form of service to the god who endowed you with many so natural gifts. How can it be just for those gifts to go unused? Where is the justice in that? You must stop avoiding leadership and see it for what it is: the opportunity for a wise man to accomplish many great and beautiful things. As leader you will be able to serve the gods by using your authority to inculcate habits of piety in the people. Remember how the people loved Tatius although he was a foreign ruler, and how they accorded divine honors to the memory of Romulus. And who knows if the people, after all their victories, are not weary of war and sated with the spoils of war? They may well be ready for a gentle leader and friend of* **Justice**, *someone who will give them good laws and a durable peace. But failing all that, even if the Romans possess an uncontrollable and maniacal lust for war,* **would it not be better to control the direction of their fury once you hold the reins of power** *and to forge bonds of goodwill and friendship between your native land and the entire Sabine race and this growing and powerful city?*

Accompanying these arguments, it is said, there were a number of auspicious omens as well as the zealous entreaties of his fellow citizens who, upon learning the purpose of the ambassadors' visit, begged him to accept the kingship as a means of restoring the peace and uniting the two cities.

NOTES

Being content with what you have: The Greek *autarkeia* was much debated in classical Greek philosophy and gives us the political and economic term *autarky*, the idea that a society can exist on its own resources.

Justice: Plutarch uses the proper noun here, *Dike*, the daughter of Zeus.

Would it not be better to control the direction of their fury once you hold the reins of power: Compare this argument with Plato's discussion in the *Republic* (7, 517-520) for why a philosopher might be persuaded to abandon his contemplative life and enter the political arena.

[7] Finally persuaded to accept the kingship, Numa sacrificed to the gods and made his way to Rome. The Senate and the people came out with great eagerness and anticipation to meet him, the women, too, welcoming him with loud acclamations. Sacrifices were made in all the temples; indeed, the rejoicing was so universal that it seemed not only a new king, but a new kingdom, was being proclaimed. In this manner he proceeded to the forum where Spurius Vettius, the man at that time appointed to the interregnum, asked the citizens to vote, and all approved. The royal insignia were then brought out to him, but he bid them hold off, saying that he needed to ask the gods to confirm his kingship. Taking the **augurs** and priests with him, he mounted the Capitolium, which the Romans at that time called the Tarpeian Rock. Then the chief augur turned to the south with his head covered. Numa, standing behind him with his right hand clasping his own head, offered a prayer and looked in every direction searching for birds or **prodigies** as signs from the gods. A sudden and awesome hush fell over the crowd as they too, full of suspense, scanned the skies for a sign until good birds on the right appeared, breaking the spell. Then Numa, after clothing himself in the royal robes, descended into the crowd from the citadel and was greeted with loud shouts and acclamations as the holiest of men, the most beloved of the gods.

His first act as king was to disband the corps of three hundred spearmen called the *Celeres*, or the Swift, that served as **Romulus' bodyguard**. This he did while saying, "I will not distrust those who have put their trust in me, nor will I rule over those who distrust me." At the same time he added a third priest for Romulus next to those of Jupiter and Mars. He called this priest the **Flamen Quirinalis**. The Romans called their earliest priests *Flamenes* owing to the felt caps (Gk. *piloi*) that covered their heads and caused them, according to their account, to be called Pilamenes. In those days, more Greek terms were incorporated into Latin than nowadays. Juba says that the *laenae* (woolen mantles) worn by the priests were originally called *chlainai* (woolen mantles in Greek). He also says that Camillus, the name given to the boy with living parents who served the *flamen dialis* (priest of Jove), derives from one of Hermes' Greek names, Cadmilos, designating one who waits on the gods.

NOTES

Augurs: Augurs were an important college of priests in Rome who read the signs in the sky, which Roman religion called a *templum* (the origin of our "temple") before any undertaking of significance, which for a Roman meant virtually any public act. The description that follows gives us a good idea of how it worked. It is interesting, however, to compare Livy's description (*A.U.C.* I.18) of this same event, where the auspices are conducted by the augur, who then prays with his right hand on Numa's head.

Prodigies: Plutarch is using the Greek word *symboloi* to translate the Latin *prodigia*, or prodigies, meaning "natural phenomena interpreted as signs from heaven," not as now understood as "every parent's children."

Romulus' bodyguard: Dionysus of Halicarnassus says that Numa did not disband the *Celeres*, and both he and Livy have them in service until the end of the monarchy. Generals (Latin *Praetores*) sometimes used elite troops as bodyguards in the Republican period and Augustus restored a permanent corps attached to his person using the Republican name *Praetorians*. The Praetorian Guard inevitably played a political role in times of crisis in the Imperial period, becoming involved in disputes over succession. They were finally disbanded after their defeat in the Battle of the Milvian Bridge by Constantine in AD 312.

Flamen Quirinalis: The *flamen quirinalis* was one of the *flamines maiores*, along with the *flamen dialis* (of Jove) and the *flamen martialis* (of Mars), the highest ranking religious officials after the *rex sacrorum*. The Latinate explanation for the word "flamen" to designate this priesthood, deriving it from a Latin root meaning blaze or flame, is generally accepted. In his text that follows, however, Plutarch offers Greek origins for Latin words connected with this priesthood.

[8] Having instituted these measures and won the good will and affection of the people, Numa immediately set about the task of converting the harsh, iron, warlike temper of the city into something more gentle and just. Never was there a city that answered more aptly to Plato's description of **"a city in a state of fever"** than Rome at that time. Founded from its very beginning by adventurous and warlike men gathered from all corners of the earth, it nurtured itself and grew by constant warfare and by preying on its neighbors. It found in conflict the source of its vitality, and like a stake that is planted more firmly the more you strike it, Rome seemed to grow stronger with each threat to its existence. Realizing how difficult it would be to make such a violent and tempestuous people peace-loving, Numa sought the help of the gods. He did this by establishing regular religious holidays with sacrifices, processions, and dances over which he often personally presided. By combining solemn rituals with enjoyable and civilized activities in this manner, he gradually won the people over and tamed their wild and warlike spirits. He also sometimes used reports of dire warning from the gods and strange apparitions of demons and threatening voices to humble the people and to fill them with religious awe and make them afraid of offending the gods.

These methods gave rise to the idea that Numa kept company with Pythagoras whose philosophy, like Numa's policies, emphasized man's relation with the gods. It is also said that he clothed and comported himself in the solemn and majestic style of Pythagoras, and for the same reasons. They claim that Pythagoras taught an eagle to stop mid-flight and come at his beckoning and that as he walked through the festive crowds at Olympia he exposed his golden thigh. These and many other amazing, conjuring acts inspired **Timon of Phlius** to write:

> *Pythagoras with his high holy preaching ensnares men,*
> *Luring them astray with his sorcerer's tricks.*

NOTES

"A city in a state of fever": *Republic* 372e (Trans. Sterling and Scott. Norton, 1996. P.68.) Plutarch finds Plato's phrase apt even if the context in the *Republic*—in Socrates' description, Glaucon's "luxurious city"—does not apply.

Timon of Phlius: A Hellenistic philosopher and satirist upon whom Shakespeare's *Timon of Athens* is based.

For Numa these acts took the form of reports about his love affair with a goddess or mountain nymph, as already mentioned, and his familiar relations with the Muses. Indeed, he attributed most of his prophecies to the Muses, and one in particular he singled out and taught the Romans to worship. He called this one Tacita, the Silent, probably another echo of **Pythagorean reserve**. Numa's law governing images also reflects the doctrines of Pythagoras, who conceived the First Being as neither perceptible nor subject to passion, but rather uncreated, infinite, and apprehended only by the intellect. Accordingly, Numa would not allow the Romans to represent their gods, whether in paintings or statues, as either men or beasts. For the first 170 years, Roman temples and shrines contained no images, and it was considered a sacrilege to draw comparisons between higher and lower beings or to conceive of the gods other than by abstract thought. Finally, even the sacrificial practices of the early Romans were like Pythagorean rites, conducted with barley, wine, and other inexpensive items rather than animals.

Besides these similarities, there are some who claim that the two men were close friends. One such is the claim made by the comic poet Epicharmus, an ancient devotee of the Pythagorean school, in a book dedicated to Antenor, that the Romans conveyed citizenship on Pythagoras. Another is the observation that King Numa named one of his four sons Mamercus after Pythagoras' son. (It is from this son, they claim, that the ancient patrician family of the Aemilii originated. The king nicknamed this boy Aemylia [Gentle in Greek] because of his gentle and graceful way of speaking.) And finally, I have had many Romans tell me that when an oracle once bid them build two monuments, one to the bravest and another to the wisest of the Greeks, they erected two bronze statues in the forum, one to Alcibiades and another to Pythagoras. But this is all a matter of debate and to persist in the defense of this claim is just childish one-upsmanship.

[9] They also attribute to Numa the institution and hierarchy of their chief priests, called ***pontifices***, of whom he was one of the first. The name pontifices, some say, derives from ***potens***, meaning powerful, because they serve the

NOTES

Pythagorean reserve: *Echemythia*, the ability to hold one's tongue, was recognized as a Pythagorian technical term.

Pontifices: The origin of the title Pontiff used of the pope in the Roman Catholic Church.

Potens: The etymology is imagined coming from *potifices*, a combination of *posse* (to be able or powerful, *potens*) and *facere* (to do).

puissant lords of the universe. Others insist that the word means something like **"what is possible."** The priests' duty was to perform all possible rites, but if something should prevent them from doing so, it would not be held against them. But **most assign the most ridiculous of origins to the word**. Since the Latin word for bridge is *pontem*, they call their priests bridge-makers. One of the oldest and most sacred rites is performed on the bridge, making it the responsibility of the priests to maintain the bridge in good repair. Possibly for this reason is the destruction of the bridge not only declared unlawful, but believed to be a downright sacrilege. They also believe that in obedience to an oracle **the bridge is built entirely of wood** and held together not with iron nails and hinges, but with wooden pegs. A stone bridge was not built on this spot until many years later under the quaestership of Aemilius. And as if this were not confusion enough, there are also those who say that no wooden bridge existed in Numa's day and that the bridge was completed in the reign of Marcius, his daughter's son.

The office of Pontifex Maximus, or chief priest, **proclaimed and interpreted** the laws of the gods and served primarily as the hierophant in charge of public ceremonies, as well as responsible for regulating private acts of oblation to prevent departure from established practice and for teaching everyone how to honor and pray correctly to the divinity. He was also in charge of the Vestal Virgins and entrusted them with the keeping of the eternal flame, either because he thought it fit for chaste and unpolluted women to keep the pure and incorruptible flame or because he saw a similarity between virginity and fire that consumes but produces nothing. Wherever in Greece a perpetual fire is maintained, as at Delphi and Athens, it is not virgins, but widows past child-bearing years, who tend the flame. If by chance the flame ever goes out—as is said to have happened to the holy lamp in Athens during the tyranny of Ariston, as well as at Delphi, both when the temple was torched by the **Maides** and later during the Mithridatic and Roman civil war when not only the flame was extinguished but the altar demolished—it cannot be relit from another fire source, but

NOTES

"What is possible": This explanation again follows an etymology from *potifices* (see note above), but it is less plausible in Latin and seems to depend on the Greek use of *dunaton*, meaning that which is possible.

Most assign the most ridiculous of origins to the word: As do modern linguists . . .

The bridge is built entirely of wood: The wooden bridge is the *Pons Sublicius*, which was preserved until the end of the Empire. The *Pons Aemilius*, or Aemilian Bridge, next to it was built from 179 to 184 BC in the censorship of Aemilius according to Livy (*A.U.C.* 40.51). The old bridge was allowed to stand for religious purposes.

Proclaimed and interpreted: Plutarch uses Greek religious terms, which are still used in traditional Christian churches. Here we have used "proclaimed" to describe the role of the prophet and "interpreted" the role of exegete. In their ancient usage, an exegete and prophet had similar functions, both proclaiming and interpreting the will of the gods through omens, dreams, oracles, etc. In modern usage an exegete interprets Holy Scripture, and the word "prophet" gained its modern sense of preacher and predictor of future events in the *Koine* Greek of the New Testament by assimilation with Hebrew prophets. As is clear from Plutarch's text here, a *hierophant* declares and protects correct conduct of sacred rites.

Maides: A Thracian tribe allied to Rome in the First Mithridatic War (89-85 BC). It is believed that Spartacus, who led the slave revolt (73-71 BC), was a Maide.

the new flame must come pure and untainted directly from the sun. They use concave mirrors to achieve this effect. Their curvature is constructed from a disc of isosceles triangles meeting at one point in the middle. When placed facing the sun, the triangles capture and direct all the rays of the sun to the center where they disperse the air and quickly kindle the fine dry combustible material placed there. Some think that the Vestal Virgins do nothing but keep the eternal flame, while others believe that they keep hidden other divine secrets and holy objects not meant to be told or seen. In my life of Camillus I have written all that it is permissible to ask or tell about these things.

[10] Getania and Verenia were the first two vestal virgins consecrated by Numa. They were followed by Canuleia and Tarpeia. King Servius later added two more to their number, bringing the total to six. Numa established the following rules for the vestals: Their vow of virginity was to last for thirty years. In the first ten years they studied the duties they were expected to perform; in the next ten years they did what they had learned; and in the last ten they taught. After completing this cycle, they were released from their vows and free to give up the priesthood, marry, and turn to another life. But only a few, they say, took advantage of this freedom, or found happiness in their new life. Instead, they spent their lives in shame and regret, and by their sad example strengthened the religious scruples and fears of the other vestals who typically kept their vows and remained virgins until old age and death. Numa granted the vestals extraordinary honors, including **the right to own and dispose of property while their father was still alive** and to manage their own affairs without being assigned a guardian, a privilege otherwise reserved for mothers with **three or more children**. When they leave their quarters, they have the **fasces** carried before them, and if on their walks they should encounter a criminal being led to execution, he is allowed to live so long as the vestal can swear that their meeting was by accident and not prearranged. By the same token, if anyone crowds or jostles the chair on which a vestal is being carried, he will be put to death.

NOTES

The right to own and dispose of property while their father was still alive: Normally a father as head of the household, *paterfamilias* in Latin, maintained exclusive property rights. His rights included the right to kill his children or sell them into slavery, but he could not disinherit them. See section [17]. According to Dionysus of Halicarnassus (*Antiquitates Romanae* 2.27.1-2), upon whom Plutarch relies for much of his information about Numa, a father had the right to sell his child into slavery as many as three times. Do you wonder how this was possible? Well, it was possible because of the common practice of Roman masters to free their slaves. When a son sold into slavery was freed by his master, "ownership" reverted once again to his father who had the right to sell him again. This could be repeated up to three times after which the son was no longer under the control of his father and was, at last, free.

Three or more children: Plutarch is referring to the Augustan legislation meant to encourage Roman women to have more than two children. Roman inheritance law divided property between living heirs, and the vast majority of marriages were arranged so as to keep property within the extended family. The Augustan legislation was meant to counteract the natural tendency to limit the dispersion of a family's estate by having only one or two children to inherit. [As a side note, French inheritance law is virtually identical, and financial incentives are granted for having more than two children, which at least in part explains why the birthrate in France tends to outpace most other wealthy European countries.]

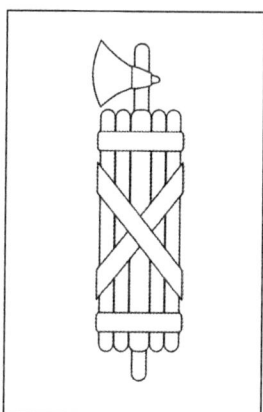

Fasces: The fasces was a bound bundle of sticks topped by an axe head. It was carried before a Roman legion on the march and symbolized the strength of the army or the state when all soldiers or citizens are united and serve a common purpose. In modern times, the fasces became a symbol for fascism.

For minor faults, the vestals are punished by the Pontifex Maximus who canes them while they stand naked behind a fine linen curtain in a dark place. But the vestal who breaks her vow is buried alive near the **Collina Gate** where within the city there is a small earthen mound called an *agger* [rampart] in Latin. Dug out under this mound is a small room with a ladder leading down to it. Inside is placed a bed with a blanket and a lit lamp, and because they do not want to starve a body consecrated to the holiest of rites, they provide a few provisions like bread, milk, oil, and a pitcher of water. The offender herself is placed inside a litter entirely enclosed and sealed with leather so that no sound she makes can be heard as she is carried through the forum. The people silently disperse as her litter passes or follow it in solemn and **dreadful** silence. There is no day more terrible, no day more mournful for the city. When the litter arrives at the place, the litter bearers loosen the seals while the chief priest prays silently with his hands outstretched to the gods. He then pulls the veiled vestal from the litter and places her on the ladder leading down to the underground room. At this point, he and the other priests turn away and leave the scene. The ladder is pulled up once the vestal has gone down, and earth is heaped up over the entrance until it is on a level with the rest of the mound. This is the punishment for the vestal who violates her vow of virginity.

[11] Numa is said to have given the temple of Vesta guarding the eternal flame its circular wall. This shape is not meant to symbolize the round earth as a *Vesta* (Latin meaning hearth), but it represents the entire universe at the center of which, according to the Pythagoreans, is the fire they call the Vesta, or **Monad**. They do not consider the earth to be immobile or to be located at the center of the universe. It moves instead in a circle around a fiery element at the center. Nor do they believe that the earth is the most important or primary element in the universe. In this they share the opinion of Plato, who, as he grew older, came to view the earth as occupying a secondary place in the universe, the central and sovereign place belonging to a nobler element.

Collina Gate: The Porta Collina is a gate in the Servian wall at the end of the Quirinal behind the ruins today of the Baths of Diocletian. [See map of Rome.]

Dreadful: The word translated by "dreadful" here is the adjective *deinos* in Greek, a word which can also be translated "awesome, awful, dreadful, or wonderful" depending on the context. In all cases it might help to remember that the English words, which we tend to use casually (and meaninglessly), all originally expressed a sense of true awe and wonder in the presence of a religious mystery. This sense is captured in the description of St. Paul's conversion when he was struck by a divine light on the road outside Damascus "and fell to the ground . . . in fear and trembling" (Acts 9: 4-6). Students of Greek might also be familiar with a famous use of the term in Sophocles' *Polla ta deina* choral ode in the Antigone: "Many the dreadful / wonderful things, and nothing more dreadful / wonderful than Man . . ."

Monad: A Monad is a unit in Greek and its usage has a long history in philosophy, theology, mathematics, and physics. In the modern world, notably the early-eighteenth-century German mathematician and philosopher Gottfried Leibniz adopted it to name his philosophical treatise *Monadology* (1720). While its meaning is distinct, contemporary cosmologists' use of "singularity" to describe black holes is linguistically similar to the Pythagoreans' use.

View of the Temple of Vesta, 1774: Etching by Jean Jacques de Boissieu, *The Met. (Public Domain Image)*

[12] A further role of the priests was to educate the people concerning appropriate rituals for funerals and burials. In this regard, Numa taught that the treatment of the dead was not a source of pollution, but rather a way of honoring the gods of the underworld who receive our **most sovereign elements**. This applied especially to the goddess they call Libitina, who presides over the holy ceremonies for the dead. She is either their name for Persephone or, as well-educated Romans believe, Aphrodite, thereby attributing to the same deity the power over both birth and death. Numa fixed the period of mourning as well, basing it on the age of the departed. For children under three years old, there was no mourning at all, and for those over three, the months of mourning matched the age of the departed up to a maximum of ten. Ten months was also the prescribed period of mourning for widows. The widow who remarried before her period of mourning was up, according to Numa's laws, sacrificed a cow carrying a calf.

Numa set up several other priesthoods as well. I shall mention two of these, the Salii and Fetiales, both offering the most convincing proofs of his piety. The **Fetiales**, or guardians of peace, take their name from their *raison d'être* as negotiators to resolve conflicts through discussion and prevent the city from going to war before all hopes of a peaceful settlement are exhausted. That is why the Greeks call it peace when differences are settled by words rather than by force. The Romans would send the Fetiales to those who in some way had injured them and persuade them to make things right. If they refuse, the Fetiales call upon the gods to bear witness, and calling baleful curses down upon themselves and the Romans if their demands should prove unjust, they declare war. Against the will or without the approval of the Fetiales, it was against the law for a king or even a single Roman soldier to take up arms. Only after receiving the Fetiales' declaration of a just war was the commander at liberty to ready his troops for battle.

NOTES

Most sovereign elements: "Our most sovereign elements"—*ta kyriotata* in Greek—is a Platonic expression designating the soul.

Fetiales: Thought to derive from the Greek word *phemi*, meaning to speak.

It is believed that the sack and destruction of their city by the Gauls happened when the Romans transgressed these sacred laws. When the barbarian Gauls were laying siege to Clusium, the Romans sent Fabius Ambustus to their camp as an ambassador to negotiate a peace for the besieged. Upon receiving their rude refusal and assuming he had fulfilled his role as an ambassador, he behaved like a hot-headed youth, took up arms for the Clusians, and challenged the bravest of the Gauls to single combat. Fortune favored Fabius, and he offed his opponent and stripped him of his armor. Seeing this, the Gauls sent a herald to Rome, accusing Fabius of having started a war against them in violation of a sworn truce and without a formal declaration. The Fetiales argued before the Senate that Fabius should be turned over to the Gauls, but before the Senate could act, Fabius took refuge with the people who supported him and prevented this sentence from being carried out. Shortly afterwards, the Gauls attacked and sacked the city, all of it except the Capitolium. I have related these events in more detail in my life of Camillus.

[13] The priesthood of the Salii began thus: In the eighth year of Numa's reign, a terrible plague ravaged all of Italy including Rome. The situation seemed hopeless and the people had grown desperate when a bronze shield suddenly fell from the sky into Numa's hands. The king gave this marvelous account of it, saying he had learned from Egeria and the Muses that the shield was sent from heaven to save the city and that eleven copies of it should be made, each so identical to the original in size and shape that a thief would not be able to tell which one was sent by the god. Numa further declared that the meadow where he was in the habit of consulting with the Muses and where the shield fell from heaven should be consecrated to the Muses. The spring watering this meadow he presented to the Vestal Virgins, who came each day to fetch its sacred water and use it to cleanse and purify their temple. In the eyes of the Romans, the sudden halting of the plague validated Numa's account.

NOTES

Bronze shield boss with griffin and sphinx frieze, ca. 650 BC
The Met. (Public Domain Image)

Numa produced the heaven-sent shield and invited Rome's finest craftsmen to compete in making exact copies of it. Everyone eventually gave up, except for a skilled armorer named Valerius Mamurius who persevered and made copies so perfect that not even Numa could tell one from the other. To guard and care for these shields, Numa then established the Salii priesthood. Some wrongly believe that the Salii received their name from Salius, a dancing master from Samothrace or Mantinea, who was the first to teach a way of dancing in armor. But in fact the name refers to the leaping dance performed by the **Salii** every **March** as they process through the city carrying the sacred shields. They wear bronze helmets and short purple tunics with wide belts studded in bronze, and they beat their shields with short swords. The dance itself involves intricate and graceful footwork with rapidly changing circular movements and impressive displays of strength and agility. The shields are called **ancilia** owing to their shape, since they are not round, nor do they describe an arc like the **pelte**. Instead their sides are convex and their corners rounded and turned in to meet at the thickest part and form an inverted curve, or in Greek *angkylos*. The name might also come from *angkōn*, or elbow, the body part to which it is attached. So says **Juba**, eager to make it appear Greek. Then again it might owe its name to the fact that it fell from on high [*anaschesis*], or from the healing [*akesis*] of the sick, or from the cessation [*anaschesis*] of the plague, a word that is also, by the way, the origin of *Anakes*, the Athenian name for Castor and Pollux. Enough of Greek etymologies!

Mamurius' reward for his technical skill is a mention in the song the Salii sing while dancing with their shields through the city. Then again, there are those who say that they are not singing "*Valerium Mamuriam*" but rather "*veterem memoriam*," meaning "ancient memory."

[14] Having established several orders of priests, Numa built the Regia, a royal palace of sorts, near the temple of Vesta. He spent most of his time there, performing sacred rituals, instructing the priests, and conversing with them about the gods. He had another house on the Quirinal, built on

NOTES

Salii: As Varro says in his *de lingua latina*, that Salii comes from *salitare*, to leap. The Greek word Plutarch uses, "*haltike*," he evidently recognizes as similar in origin.

March: The month of March being named after Mars, the Roman god of war. Before Julius Caesar revised the calendar in 45 BC, the Roman year began in March, when newly elected officials assumed their functions and (before a permanent army was created in the first century BC) citizens were called up for military service on the Field of Mars and the campaigning season began.

Ancilia: See the Greek *angkylos* below. Both words come from a common root from which we get the word "angle" for example. [See illustration.]

Pelte: A small leather shield, sometimes called a "target" in English.

Juba: Perhaps Juba of Mauretania, a contemporary of Plutarch, who wrote a treatise on meter.

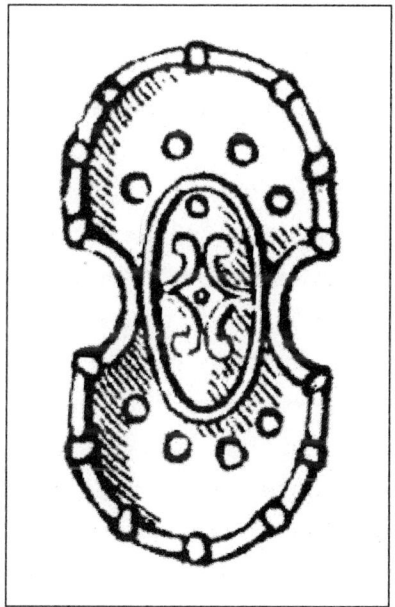

Ancilia Shield

a site the Romans still point out. Before public prayers and religious processions, heralds were sent out to instruct the people to keep quiet and stop working. It is said that the Pythagoreans were not allowed to worship and pray to the gods casually or with a **gesture as they passed** their shrines and temples, but were expected to leave their houses and proceed directly to the house of worship with the intention of worship in mind. Likewise, Numa did not want his citizens to see or hear any religious observance without giving it their full attention. Rather they were expected to cease all activities and concentrate exclusively on the most important activity of all, namely piety, and in preparation for the sacred rituals they were to cleanse the streets of all the crying, groaning, banging, and other noises that usually accompany manual labor. A trace of this custom survives in Rome to this day. When a magistrate is about to take auspices or make a sacrifice, he will cry out, *Hoc age!* meaning "Be attentive!" as a way of calling upon those in the vicinity to stop what they are doing and act properly.

Many of Numa's precepts resembled those of the Pythagoreans, who said, for example, "Do not sit on an urn full of grain. Do not stir a fire with a sword. Do not turn back once you have set out on a trip. Sacrifice an odd number of victims to the celestials gods and an even number to the terrestrial or chthonic gods." No explanation was given for these precepts, and sometimes they contained hidden meanings. For example, Numa insisted that no libation to the gods should be made with wine from an un-pruned vine, that no sacrifice should be made without flour, and that the worshipper should turn once around when paying adoration to the gods and then sit down. Now, the first two of these instructions appear to identify the cultivation of the land with religious observance, while the turning around of the third is said to represent the rotation of the earth. To me it seems more likely that since the worshipper enters from the west the temple facing east, he honors the god in every direction by turning in a full circle. Unless, by Zeus! Numa is suggesting some mysterious connection with the Egyptian **wheel of fate** whereby turning represents the instability and unpredictability of human life, and however the god chooses to turn and unfold our lives we

NOTES

Gesture as they passed: Ancient cities were full of temples and shrines, which people would customarily acknowledge by a religious gesture or prayer in passing, as is the case today in traditional countries.

Wheel of fate: Clement of Alexandria describes how Egyptian priests gave flowers and a wheel, as symbols of change and instability, to those who came to their temples to pray. The worshipper turned the wheel during prayer.

should be grateful and accept it as just and right. As for sitting after worship, they say it shows confidence that the god will answer our prayers. We can *rest* assured. It is also possible that just as one pauses after completing one action and before beginning another, the worshipper sits after completing his prayer to receive the god's blessing and guidance before going on to something else. All of this makes sense, of course, and agrees with Numa's general concern, expressed earlier, that his citizens should not approach the gods casually as if in a hurry or with other business on their minds, but when they can slow down and give the god their undivided time and attention.

[15] All of this religious education made the Romans credulous, not to say gullible, and placed them under Numa's spell to the point that they came to accept the most preposterous stories as true and believe nothing he said was incredible or propose impossible. There is a story, for example, about how he once invited a large number of citizens to dine with him, and he placed before them a very humble meal on cheap serving dishes. His guests began to eat when all of a sudden he announced that the goddess with whom he consorted had just arrived. At once the room was furnished with priceless drinking cups and tables laden with expensive meats and other delicacies, all served on magnificent platters.

But by far the most absurd story is the one about his conversation with Jupiter. Legend has it that two demi-gods, Faunus and Picus, were in the habit of visiting the Aventine, a hill possessing many springs and shady glens and not yet settled and inside the city walls. They were probably satyrs or belonged to the race of Titans. Whatever they were, through the use of powerful potions or conjuring tricks they pulled off throughout Italy the same sorts of metallurgical feats the Greeks ascribe to the **Dactyls** on Mount Ida. The Romans say that one day Numa gained power over them by mixing wine and honey in the waters of the spring from which they came to drink. They tried to escape Numa's control by taking many different forms and changing into strange and terrifying apparitions. Once they realized, however, that they were securely bound and could not

Dactyls: In Greek mythology there are many stories about the Dactyls, among them the claim that they were metallurgists employed in Hephaistos' workshop. While Rhea was suffering contractions giving birth to Zeus (Jupiter) in a cave on Mount Ida, she dug her fingers into the earth (Gaia) from which sprang the ten Dactyls (also in English, fingers). Pausanias 5.7.6 tells us that Rhea made the Dactyls the guardians of her son, interesting in light of this story's connection with Jove.

escape, they revealed many secrets and predicted many future events. In particular, they taught Numa the ceremony for purification after **lightning strikes**, a rite involving onions, hair, and whitebait that is still practiced. But some tell a different story, saying that Faunus and Picus did not teach him the purification ceremony but used their magic to bring down ("elicit") Jove. The angered god ordered Numa to accomplish the purification with heads.

> "Heads of onions?" asked Numa.
> "Of men!" said Jove.
> Trying to deflect such a dreadful command and change the subject, Numa answered, "Ah, you mean with the hairs of their heads."
> "No!" Jove replied. "I mean living . . .
> ". . . whitebait!" Numa interjected, having been told by Egeria to say this.
> So Jove returned to heaven propitiated [ileōs], and the Romans call the place where this happened **Ilicius**, and the purification ceremony is performed in this way.

These fabulous fables that now seem ridiculous reveal the power that religion held over the people of Numa's time. Numa himself is said to have had so much confidence in his religious beliefs that when a messenger once warned him that enemies were approaching, he answered him, smiling, "And I am sacrificing."

[16] Numa also built the temples to Faith [*Fides*] and Terminus and taught the Romans that the strongest oath they could swear was by Faith. Today, they still swear by Faith. To the god Terminus, or Boundary, they make public and private sacrifices on the borders of their fields. These sacrifices are now made with animals, but in ancient times they were made without the shedding of blood because Numa reasoned that the god of boundaries, who guarded the peace and protected property rights, should be untainted by slaughter. Numa, clearly, was the first king to mark the boundaries of

Lightning strikes: Scholars are not certain of what this means. Perhaps lightning strikes, as indications of Jupiter's anger, required an act of propitiation to avoid the god's wrath. Or perhaps the purification ceremony was meant to call forth rain, usually but not necessarily associated with lightning. Jupiter is no doubt loath to share his absolute control of thunder and lightning with a mere mortal. Is there something Promethean about Numa in this tale?

Ilicius: The Romans (cf. Ovid, *Fastes* 3) called this the sanctuary of *Juppiter Elicius* on the Aventine and derived the epithet from the Latin *elicio*, from which we get "elicit" since it was a place where Jupiter could be asked to come down to earth.

Roman territory. Romulus never did this for fear it would show how much land he had taken from his neighbors. Nevertheless, boundaries provide a good defense if others honor them and a proof of injustice against those who trespass. In fact, the Romans possessed very little territory in the beginning, and Romulus greatly extended it in war.

Numa tried to eliminate poverty by distributing the territory taken by Romulus among the poorest of Rome's citizens. He did this in the belief that poverty was an inevitable source of discontent and unrest and that turning the poor into farmers would improve both the state and the land. Nothing cultivates contentment and a love of peace like farming and the country life. At the same time, it makes men courageous and ready to fight in defense of their own lands while cutting short the ambitions of those who wish to trespass and take what is not theirs. In this way Numa viewed agriculture as a means of pacifying the people, valuing it more for its affect on their character than as a producer of wealth. He divided all the land into parcels which he called **pagi**, and he assigned an overseer to each *pagus*. He would sometimes inspect the *pagi* himself, judging the character of the farmer from his care of the land, promoting the industrious to positions of honor and trust while encouraging the indolent or careless to improve by admonishing or punishing them.

[17] The most admired of all Numa's measures was his division of the people by trade or craft. As I have already explained, a union of two tribes formed the city, or rather I should say *a division* of two tribes. The fact that each tribe remained wedded to its own customs and characteristics and preferred them to those of the other was a constant source of conflict and civil strife. Numa, likening this situation to two solid and brittle blocks that could not be combined, conceived the idea of breaking up the blocks into small particles that could then be easily mixed together. He divided the entire population into several smaller groups, thereby introducing new group identities and distinctions that obliterated the original and great distinction. The new division was made according to trades and crafts: musicians,

Pagi: Country folk, e.g., those who lived in the *pagi*, were accordingly called in Latin *pagani*, the origin of our word "pagans"—the name given by early (generally urban) Christians to non-believers who were backward, lived in the country, and held to their traditional religions.

goldsmiths, carpenters, dyers, shoemakers, tanners, blacksmiths, and potters. Each craft he formed into a single guild and assigned to each a meeting place, governing body, and suitable set of religious rituals. From this time the city's factions began to disappear and the citizens stopped thinking of themselves as Sabines or Romans, Tatius' men or Romulus', and the guilds became a source of Rome's harmony and unification.

Numa should also be praised for amending the law that gave fathers the right to sell their children. He exempted married persons from this law, so long as they were married at their father's command or with his consent. It seemed unfair to him that a woman who married a man who at the time of their marriage was free should later find herself living with a **slave**.

[18] Numa also revised the Roman calendar. Although not perfect, his revisions revealed a somewhat scientific understanding of the heavens. During the time of Romulus, there was no rhyme or reason to the way the Romans measured their months. Some contained twenty days, some thirty-five days, and others still more. They had no idea of how to coordinate lunar and solar cycles, and maintained only that a year consisted of 360 days. Calculating that the difference between the lunar year (354 days) and the solar year (365 days) is eleven days, Numa added an additional month containing twenty-two days every other year after the month of February. The Romans call this intercalary month Mercedinus. (This remedy afterwards required even further refinements.) He changed the order of the months. He moved March, which had been the first month, to third place. January, which was the eleventh month in Romulus' time, he moved to first place. And February, which had been the twelfth month, he moved to second place. Many claim that Numa added the months of January and February and that before his time the Roman calendar contained only ten months, not unlike some barbarians who count as few as three months in a year. Then there are the Greeks among whom the Arcadians recognize four months and the Arcananians six. It is said that the Egyptian calendar contained only one month at first, and later four. Because their months are

NOTES

Slave: This passage implies that under the old law, the paterfamilias, so long as he lived, had the right to sell his children into slavery even after they had married.

counted as years, the lineage of Egypt's inhabitants is reckoned to be very ancient and their genealogies extend back an impossible number of years.

[19] The fact that the Romans still call the last month of the year **December**, meaning the tenth month, proves that their year contained ten months, not twelve. **Quintilis**, the name of the fifth month after March, likewise proves that March was the first month. And after that **Sextilis**, meaning sixth, and so on until December. When they placed January and February before March, they continued to call what became the seventh month by the name of the fifth. Nor is it surprising that during the time of Romulus, the Romans placed March, the month sacred to the god Mars, first.

April, named for Aphrodite (Venus) to whom sacrifices are offered in April, was naturally placed second. On the first day of this month women bathe with garlands of myrtle in their hair. There are those who dispute this explanation, saying that **April** is not named for Aphrodite because it is spelled with a *p* rather than a *ph*. They claim the word derives from *aperire*, meaning to open, since this is the month when spring reaches its climax and buds and blossoms open and flower. May comes next, from Maïa, the mother of Mercury, to whom this month is sacred. Then follows June, named after **Juno**. It is believed by some that these two months are eponyms for old age and youth, since *maiores* in Latin designates older men and *juniores* younger ones.

The rest of the months take their names from their order in the calendar: fifth (Quintilis), sixth (Sextilis), seventh (Septembris), eighth (Octobris), ninth (Novembris), and tenth (Decembris). The fifth month, as noted above, was named Julius for Caesar who defeated Pompey; and the eighth month for Augustus, meaning reverend or venerable, who ruled after him. Wishing to do the same or one better, Domitian imposed his surnames on the next two months, Germanicus and Domitianus, but after he was assassinated they reverted back to Septembris and Octobris. Only the last two months have from the beginning kept their names from their order in the calendar.

NOTES

December: *Decembris* is tenth in Latin.

Quintilis: Meaning fifth and renamed July after Julius Caesar, as explained later in this chapter.

Sextilis: The sixth month was renamed August after Caesar Augustus.

April: *Aprilis* and not *Aphrilis* In other words, when spoken the word is not aspirated. The Greeks understood the name Aphrodite, following the poet Hesiod's account (*Theogony* II.154-206), to refer to her birth and meant "sprung-from-the-foam (*aphro*)," from which the first explanation supposes Aprilis to derive.

Juno: Juno the consort of Jupiter, from which we get the tradition of June weddings.

Of the months added or shifted by Numa, February is the month of purification, which is exactly what the word *februarius* means. At this time the Romans make offerings to the dead and celebrate the festival of the **Lupercalia** in a ritual that in many ways resembles a purification ceremony. The first month, Januarius, comes from the name Janus. Numa removed March, named for Mars, from first place because, as I believe, he wanted to give the arts of peace precedence over those of war. This Janus was thought to have ruled as a demi-god or king in remote antiquity with consummate social and political skills, which he used to transform man's bestial and savage manner of life. Having substituted one manner of life for another, he is now represented as having **two faces**.

[20] Janus' temple in Rome has two gates that they call the gates of war because they remain open in times of war and closed in times of peace. The latter was indeed a rare occurrence. Being so large and forced to fend off enemies that threatened it from every side, Rome was almost never at peace. Augustus closed the gates for a time after defeating Marc Antony. Once before that during the consulships of Marcus Atilius and Titus Mallius they were closed, but then opened almost immediately **after war broke out**. During the reign of Numa, however, the gates were not seen open for a single day, and so pervasive was the love of peace in his time that they remained shut for forty-three years without opening once. In fact it was not only the Roman people over which Numa seemed to cast his spell of gentleness and justice. As if carried on a gentle and salubrious breeze blowing from Rome, all the cities round about seemed to participate in a general longing for good government and the arts of peace, content to stay at home and farm their lands, raise their children, and worship their gods.

Festivals, banquets, and parties with friends filled all of Italy during Numa's time. Strangers enjoyed the hospitality of strangers and traveled about without fear. As though from a perpetual spring,

NOTES

Lupercalia: The Lupercalia was a very old agricultural festival celebrated in mid-February in which the city was cleansed of evil spirits. The name apparently derives from *lupus*, meaning wolf.

Two faces: Plutarch's explanation is a bit eccentric. Janus is generally understood to be an old Roman deity of beginnings, placed over doorways and entrances and watching over those going in and out. The Latin word for door, *ianua*, derives from him.

After war broke out: In the *Res Gestae Divi Augusti* (The Achievements of the Deified Augustus) Augustus is made to say that the gate, which he calls the Ianus Quinnus (probably a corruption of Ianus Quirinus, or Janus of Romulus), was closed three times during his principate and only twice before. For the brief closing after the First Punic War in 235 BC, Plutarch's consuls should read Caius Atilius Balbus and Titus Manlius Torquatus.

a peaceful calm flowed forth from Numa's wisdom that watered all the land with a longing for justice and a love of virtue, making even the **hyperboles of the poets** seem faint and understated:

> *Spiders covered the iron spears with their dark webs,*

Or

> *Now rust dulls the sword's double edge*
> *And blunts the spear's lethal point;*
> *No more the brazen bugle's blast,*
> *And sweet sleep routed from our eyes no more.*

Indeed, throughout the entire time of Numa, there was no rumor of war, riot, or revolution, nor did the king arouse out of envy, hatred, or ambition any plot or conspiracy against him. Life was untouched by evil in his day. Whether this was from fear of the gods who watched over him, or out of respect for his virtue, or by divine providence, who can say? His reign offered a shining example and proof of what Plato, who lived long after him, dared to utter about politics: that the evils suffered by mankind will only end when the **power of the king and the wisdom of the philosopher** come together in a single person to establish virtue's rule over vice.

> *The wise man is truly called blessed, and also blessed are those who hear the words flowing from the wise man's mouth.*

It is also possible that the only thing needed to make people law-abiding without the need for enforcement and fear of punishments is the brilliant and conspicuous example of a virtuous leader. Just the example of a blameless and blessed manner of life will inspire imitation and bring people together, of their own free will, to live in harmony with one another and to seek justice for all. Is this not the best outcome law and politics can

NOTES

Hyperboles of the poets: These are fragments from a paean of Bacchylides, a Greek lyric poet who was active in Magna Graecia (Sicily and Southern Italy) and the Peloponnese in the early fifth century BC.

Power of the king and the wisdom of the philosopher: The saying that Plato "dared to utter" is found in the fifth book of the *Republic*. His famous call for a philosopher-king is from the fourth book of the *Laws* where this quote is also found.

hope to achieve? The greatest ruler is the one who instills these habits and this manner of life in his people. We can pay Numa no higher compliment than to say that he understood this better than anyone ever has.

[21] Historians offer competing accounts of Numa's wives and children. Some say that he took no other wife than **Tatia** and fathered no other child besides one daughter Pompilia. Others record that he also had four sons by Tatia: Pompon, Pinus, Calpus, and Mamercus, each of whom sired children whose descendants comprise the illustrious families of the Pomponii, the Pinarii, the Calpurnii, and the Mamercii. These families have taken the surname Reges, meaning Kings. Then there is a third set of writers who dismiss these accounts as lies told by those hoping to ingratiate themselves with these families by inventing genealogies that trace their roots back to Numa. They claim that Pompilia was not the daughter of Tatia, but of another woman named Lucretia whom he married while king. Whatever the case, everyone agrees that Pompilia married the son of the same Marcius who persuaded him to accept the kingship and moved with him to Rome where he was given a seat in the senate. After Numa died, he competed with Tullus Hostilius for the kingship, and perhaps feeling dishonored for having lost the election, he lost interest and simply wasted away. Meanwhile, his son, also named Marcius, continued to live in Rome with Pompilia and sired a son, Ancus Marcius, who became king after Hostilius. (He was only five when Numa died.) Numa lived a little more than eighty years, and according to the historian Piso, he did not die from a sudden accident or acute disease, but rather he went into a gentle decline until he passed away from old age.

[22] Numa's funeral reflected the glories of his life. Representatives from the allies and friendly states neighboring Rome brought gifts and garlands to decorate his tomb. Senators bore the litter on which his corpse was laid, and the priests of the gods followed in solemn procession. The rest of the people, including women and children, accompanied the procession with

Tatia: See section [3] above.

loud wails and cries of mourning, as if they had lost a beloved family member cut down in the prime of life rather than an old and worn-out king. They did not cremate his corpse—he forbade it, so they say—but in accordance with his wishes they buried two stone coffins at the foot of the hill **Janiculum**. In one of the coffins they laid out his corpse, and in the other they placed the sacred books which he had fashioned himself in the same way the Greek lawgivers wrote their **tablets**.

While Numa was still alive he had instructed the priests in what he had written, making sure that it was written in their hearts as well as their minds. Having accomplished this and believing that it would be irreverent to allow his sacred precepts to circulate as mere **lifeless words**, he asked that the tablets be buried with him. For the same reason they say that the Pythagoreans do not write down their precepts, but entrust them instead to the living memory of those considered worthy. Once they revealed the secrets concerning a method of solving problems in geometry to someone unworthy, and for this terrible crime of defilement, they say, the god promised to send a great public calamity. Because of these similarities between Numa and Pythagoras, we should forgive those who imagine they actually knew each other.

Valerius Antias writes that there were twelve books on religion and twelve volumes of philosophy, written in Greek, in the stone coffin. He claims that four hundred years later, when Publius Cornelius and Marcus Baebius were consuls, heavy rains loosened the earth and caused flooding that exposed the coffins. When their lids were removed, one coffin was found empty, with no bones or trace of a body, and in the other they found the tablets described above. The Praetor at the time, Petilius, read the contents of the tablets and brought them to the Senate where, after swearing an oath, he said he was of the opinion that it would be a sacrilege to make the contents of the tablets known to the people. The books were then taken to the **Comitium** and burned.

It is the happy fate of all good and just men to be praised more after they are dead than when they lived. The envy of evil men never lasts long,

NOTES

Janiculum: The Janiculum is the hill overlooking Rome on the other side of the Tiber. Its name derives from Janus, and it is said to have been incorporated in the city by Ancus Marcius.

Tablets: Plutarch refers to triangular stone tablets fitted at the angles so as to form a pyramid of three sides, and having the earliest laws written on the sides.

Lifeless words: Consider this: Our first record of words being read without being spoken is in the fourth century AD when Augustine notices with amazement Bishop Ambrose reading silently to himself. Until the word is spoken (accompanied by breath) it does not live. It lies "dead" on the page. Also in antiquity, to be published meant that the work was read publicly.

Valerius Antias: Valerius Antias was a first-century BC historian whose chronicles of legendary Rome only survive in fragments found in other writers such as Livy.

Comitium: The Comitium was the meeting place of the assembly of the people in the Roman Forum.

sometimes even dying before they do. The misfortunes of the kings who followed Numa, however, burnished his reputation even more. Of the five kings who followed him, the last one fell from power and grew old in exile while none of the other four died a natural death. Three were conspired against and assassinated, and the fourth, Tullus Hostilius, who reigned after Numa, mocked and insulted most of the fine things Numa had done. He especially ridiculed Numa's devotion to religious worship, accusing it of making men cowards and leading to idleness, and he turned the hearts and minds of the people back to war. But his childish insults did not last long. Under the grave effects of debilitating illness, he resorted to superstitions that had nothing in common with the piety of Numa, and he spread the disease of superstition to others until, it is said, a bolt of lightning struck him down.

COMPARISON

*of the Lawgivers
Lycurgus and Numa*

COMPARISON

[1] Having completed the lives of Lycurgus and Numa, it is now time to consider how their lives differ. What the two have in common is obvious: their moderation, their piety, their genius for government and education, and the fact that they both traced their laws to one and the same source, the gods. Yet within the virtues they share there are marked differences. The first is that Numa took up the kingship and Lycurgus laid it down. What Numa received he did not ask for, and what Lycurgus already possessed he gave back. The one, a private citizen and foreigner, was made a sovereign and king while the other, a high and mighty king, made himself a lowly private citizen. Now, if it is a noble thing to acquire a crown owing to justice, it is even nobler to prefer justice to a crown. This same virtue that made one man appear worthy of the crown led another to disregard it.

Another difference between the two may be compared to the tuning of a lyre. Lycurgus tightened what had grown slack and soft in Sparta while Numa loosened the excessively taut and high-strung spirits of the Romans. Lycurgus' task was the harder of the two. After all, his task was not to persuade his fellow citizens to unbuckle their shields and put down their swords, but to throw away their gold and silver and throw out their costly furniture and richly-laden tables. He was not asking them to give up fighting for religious festivals and sacrifices and to forego sweating in the gym and working out clad in full armor in order to spend more time at banquets and drinking parties. It is hardly surprising, then, that owing to his gentleness, Numa was able to accomplish his task through friendly persuasion whereas Lycurgus barely succeeded in his task, and even then only after running many risks and suffering personal attacks. Numa's muse was gentle and humane, and well suited to the work of calming and civilizing a bunch of ill-tempered and hotheaded warriors and turning them into just and peace-loving citizens. And if we must include the harsh and savage measures against the helots in Lycurgus' reforms, we have to admit that Numa was by far the more humane and Greek-like of the two lawgivers.[1]

---

1. The ancient Greeks never gave up the idea that to be civilized you had to be Hellenized. In their eyes, even Romans were barbarians.

He even gave slaves a taste of liberty by seating them with their masters during the feasts of the Saturnalia.² The Romans say that this ancestral custom was Numa's way of allowing those who contributed to the year's harvest to enjoy some of its fruits. Others say that this is done in memory of the Age of Saturn,³ a Golden Age when there was neither master nor slave and all men lived as brothers and as equals.

[2] In general, they both sought to move their people in the direction of moderation and self-sufficiency. When it came to the other virtues, however, Lycurgus preferred courage, Numa justice. This difference we should probably attribute to the differences in the social and political situations they each faced. It was not out of cowardice that Numa stopped the Romans from going to war, but to keep them from committing injustices upon their neighbors. And Lycurgus was not trying to build warrior citizens that they might do injustices to others, but rather that they might prevent injustices from being done to themselves.

Changing the habits of their respective citizens—removing their excesses and supplying what they lacked—demanded change on a massive scale. In the way they catered to a citizenry composed of every class and craft, jewelers, musicians, cobblers, and the like, Numa's laws and institutions were unduly democratic. Those of Lycurgus, on the other hand, were austere and aristocratic in the extreme. They banished as base and unclean all crafts and manual labor, putting this work in the hands of household slaves and resident aliens. The only tools he allowed his citizens were shields and spears, and the only tradecraft, war and service to Ares. The only education he allowed them was training in obedience to

---

2. The Feast of the Saturnalia, held on December 17th, and extending later through December 23rd, resembled our pre-Lenten Carnival and in many ways looked forward to our Christmas festivities. Social orders and norms were overturned, gifts exchanged, and a King of the Saturnalia elected.

3. Famous ancient accounts may be found in Hesiod's *Works and Days* and in Ovid's *Metamorphoses*.

COMPARISON

their commanders and instruction in defeating their enemies. Nor were free men permitted to work for money. To make sure money matters never interested or concerned his citizens, Lycurgus turned anything having to do with money—as well as preparing food and waiting tables—over to the slaves and helots.

Numa, on the other hand, made no such distinction. He put an end to military ambition only and placed no restrictions on moneymaking. He allowed his citizens to amass as much wealth as they liked and paid no attention when this led to extremes of poverty and wealth that like bilge water seeped up throughout the city. From the very outset, when Roman inequality was slight and Romans shared the same manner of living, Numa would have been well advised to take steps, as Lycurgus did, to guard against greed and the damage it can inflict on the state. The seed of avarice may have seemed small at first, but it grew to cause all the evils that later befell Rome. As for the equal distribution of the land, I do not believe that either Lycurgus or Numa can be blamed, the one for having done it, or the other for having failed to do it after making the original distribution of Romulus' land.[4] Lycurgus made equality of ownership the cornerstone and foundation of his constitution, whereas for Numa land equality was not a principle, and there was nothing to urge a re-division of the land after his original distribution achieved its purpose of pacifying and employing the poor.

[3] Both Lycurgus and Numa advocated the sharing of wives and children as a means of preventing jealousy, but they went about it in very different ways. If approached by a childless man who came requesting his wife, a Roman who thought he had enough children could legally separate from his wife, all the while retaining the right to divorce her or take her back later. A Spartan, on the other hand, might be persuaded to loan his wife to another man for the purpose of having children while she remained at

---

4. By adding the reference to the original distribution of Romulus' land, we are taking liberty with Plutarch's text in an attempt to clear up an apparent discrepancy with what he says in Numa section [16].

THE LAWGIVERS

home and they remained legally married. As we noted earlier,[5] many men would seek out and bring home men whom they thought would give them handsome and noble children. What then distinguishes the two customs? Is it fair to say that the Spartan custom shows an extreme disregard for the woman who for many men is merely a source of jealousies and complaints, whereas the Roman custom draws the modest veil of a marriage contract over the new arrangement which both husband and wife might otherwise find difficult to endure?

Support for this conclusion can be found in the fact that Numa made a point of protecting feminine decency in young girls whereas under Lycurgus, as the poets were fond of telling, feminine decency was utterly abandoned. Ibycus called the young women of Sparta "thigh-flashers," and Euripides accused them of driving men mad, frolicking

> *Out of doors with the young men*
> *Thighs naked and skirts lifted.*[6]

The lower skirts of the girl's tunic were not sewn together on the sides and opened revealing her entire thigh as she walked. Sophocles sketches the same thing in his verses:

> *And the young girl, Hermione,*
> *Still wearing only the unstitched skirt*
> *Unfolding and baring her thigh*[7]

Because of this, they say, Spartan women grew bold and masculine, bossy with their husbands and tyrants in their households, speaking their minds freely in public even on matters of highest importance.

---

5. *Lycurgus* section [15].

6. *Andromache,* 597f.

7. Fragment 872. From a lost play of Sophocles.

149

COMPARISON

Under Numa, husbands continued to show their wives the respect and honor they had come to expect under Romulus as a sort of atonement for having been stolen in the first place. By the same token, he urged wives to comport themselves with great modesty. He forbade them from meddling, taught them sobriety, accustomed them to keep silent, to abstain entirely from wine, and never to speak on important subjects except in the presence of their husbands. In this regard, his precepts were so successful that when a woman once broke the silence to plead her own case in court, the senate sent to inquire of the oracle if this was meant as a sign of some kind from the gods. Perhaps the best proof of their gentleness and submissiveness is the record of the exceptions to this rule. Just as the Romans have carefully recorded the names of the men who first slew a family member or murdered a brother, killed his father or his mother, so they have retained the memory of the first man, Spurius Carvilius, who had to divorce his wife, something that had not happened since the founding of the city 230 years before![8] They also remember the name of the first woman who talked back to her mother-in-law: Thalia, the wife of Pinarius, who quarreled with her mother-in-law, Getania, in the reign of Tarquin the Proud.

Hard to argue with this record of the lawgiver's success in crafting ordinances that preserved orderly marriages.

[4] Their rules for when to give young girls in marriage agree with the rest of their educational philosophy. Lycurgus had them marry when they were fully grown and eager for it. By following nature in this way, he believed that sexual intercourse would strengthen the couple's feelings of love and tenderness toward each other instead of the revulsion and fear that resulted from forcing nature in a premature marriage. Moreover, since the only reason to marry was to bear children, it made sense to wait until a girl's body was strong enough to endure pregnancy and

---

8. Note that there is no question as to who was at fault. Makes you wonder what she had done!? Sipped some wine? Passed on a bit of gossip?

childbirth. The Romans, on the other hand, gave their daughters in marriage at twelve years of age and even younger. This ensured the husband of his bride's purity and innocence. Obviously, Lycurgus' concern was the bride's suitability for bearing children, whereas the Romans wanted to make sure of the marriage's moral foundation.

Measured against Lycurgus' detailed instructions for the supervision of children, their division into companies, their life in common, their education and training as well as all the attention paid to their meals, exercises, and games, Numa comes up short. Numa left all of this up to the whims and needs of the father, whether he wished to make his son a farmer or teach him carpentry, blacksmithing or flute-playing, as if there were not a general sort of learning that prepared all children for citizenship and a civilized life. Instead they were like passengers on a ship, each having chosen to be there for his own reasons and attending to his own needs. They unite for the common good only at moments of danger out of fear for themselves because they are only looking out for themselves.

This neglect of education through ignorance or weakness may be forgiven in a run-of-the-mill legislator, but in a wise man like Numa, given carte blanche and charged with sovereignty over a newly formed people, this oversight is hard to account for. What could be more important than to prevent conflicting norms and discordant forms of behavior from arising? And to do this by starting with the raising of children and the training of young people, uniting them and forming their habits around a common understanding and reverence for virtue? His attention to these details, among other things, is what preserved Lycurgus' reforms in Sparta. Regardless of the oath they had sworn to uphold Lycurgus' laws, it would have had little effect without the discipline and education that stamped a profound respect and love for his laws on the Spartan character. For over five hundred years the greatest and most important of Lycurgus' reforms endured, preserved in the temper of his people as if in a perfect quenching solution.

COMPARISON

In the case of Numa, alas, the supreme aim of all his reforms, that peace and good will should reign in Rome, died with him. He was no sooner dead than the twin-gated shrine of Janus, whose doors he had kept closed as if he could somehow keep the god of war locked up inside, flew wide open, and Mars rushed out, filling all of Italy with dead bodies and blood. And so Numa's just and noble experiment in government lasted but a moment because it lacked the one thing that might have preserved it: education.

"What! Are you saying that it would have been better for Rome not to have grown and vanquished her enemies?"

That is a question that demands a long answer and one that may not convince those who value wealth, luxury, and power more than security, benevolence, and self-sufficiency combined with justice.[9]

At the same time, and further proof of the superiority of Lycurgus' legislation, is the fact that it was by abandoning Numa's reforms that Rome was able to acquire its vast empire. The Spartans, on the other hand, tumbled from greatness to abject poverty the moment they strayed from Lycurgus' constitution. They lost their hegemony over the Greeks and were almost wiped out.

But this much must be said for Numa and make him seem almost divine: Although assuming the reins of power as a foreigner, he was by persuasion alone able to reform everything and unite a divided city. He did all this without the use of force (unlike Lycurgus, who placed the aristocrats over the people), and by the example of his wisdom and justice, he won over and harmonized all the diverse elements of Roman society.

---

9. Compare Plato's *Republic* 427e. Here we see Plutarch channeling Plato in a most explicit way.

BIBLIOGRAPHY

TEXTS

Clough, A.H., ed. *Plutarch's Lives, The Translation Called Dryden's (Vol I)*. New York and London: Harper & Brothers, 1906.

Flacelière et al. *Plutarque Vies, tome I*. 3e, tirage revu et corrigé par Jean Irigoin. Paris: Les Belles Lettres, 1993.

Waterfield, Robin. *Plutarch, Greek Lives*. Oxford: Oxford University Press, 1998.

Ziegler, Konrat. *Plutarchi Vitae parallelae*. Vol. III, fasc. 2. 2e édition. Leipzig: Teubner, 1973.

SECONDARY WORKS CITED (cited by the author's last name)

Adam, James. *The Republic of Plato, Edited with Critical Notes, Commentary and Appendices, Second Edition*. D.A. Rees. Cambridge: Cambridge University Press, 1963.

Barrow, R.H. *Plutarch and his Times*. Bloomington & London: Indiana University Press, 1967.

Forrest, W.G. *A History of Sparta*. London: Bristol Classical Press, 1995.

Lamberton, Robert. *Plutarch*. New Haven: Yale University Press, 2002.

Marrou, Henri-Irénée. *Histoire de l'éducation dans l'Antiquité*. Paris: Editions du Seuil, 1948.

Russell, D.A. *Plutarch*. New York: Charles Scribner's Sons, 1973.

de Ste. Croix, G.E.M. *The Class Struggle in the Ancient Greek World*. Ithaca: Cornell University Press, 1981.

Sterling, Richard W., and William C. Scott. Plato, *The Republic*. New York: Norton, 1985.

IMAGE CREDITS

Introduction: *The Image of the Hammurabi Stele,* Louvre Museum, Paris, France. Room 3: Mésopotamie, IIe millénaire avant J.-C. Richelieu, ground floor. Original image by Mbzt. Uploaded by Jan van der Crabben, published on 26 April 2012 under the following license: Creative Commons: Attribution-ShareAlike. http://avalon.law.yale.edu. The Avalon Project at the Yale Law School.

Unless otherwise noted, images are in the public domain and are used courtesy of Wikimedia Commons and The Met.

 The CiRCE Institute is a non-profit 501(c)3 organization that exists to promote and support classical education in the school and in the home. We seek to identify the ancient principles of learning, to communicate them enthusiastically, and to apply them vigorously in today's learning settings through curriculum development, teacher training, leadership development events, online training, and a content-laden website.

To learn more please visit circeinstitute.org.